HOPI TRADITIONAL LITERATURE

HOPI TRADITIONAL LITERATURE

DAVID LEEDOM SHAUL

University of New Mexico Press
Albuquerque

© 2002 by the University of New Mexico Press
All rights reserved.
First edition

Library of Congress Cataloging-in-Publication Data

Shaul, David Leedom.
  Hopi traditional literature / David Leedom Shaul.
    p. cm.
Includes bibliographical references and index.
  ISBN 0-8263-2009-0 (cloth : alk. paper)

  1. Hopi literature—History and criticism.   2. Hopi language—Grammar.   I. Title.
  PM1351.Z77 S53 2002
  897'.45—dc21

                              2002000567

Dedicated to the Hopi people
who have shared the public
part of their literary tradition
with the outside world.

CONTENTS

TABLES

PREFACE

THE PURPOSE OF THIS book is to describe the main genres of traditional Hopi literature. The approach taken is to treat each genre from the perspective of the structure of texts in Hopi. Thus, reference must be made to Hopi grammar, although no knowledge of linguistics or discourse analysis is assumed. Technical terms are set off in bold face when they first occur and are explained in the text as well as in the glossary. I have tried to keep the technical discussion as clear and concise as possible.

In many ways this work is a rhetoric of Hopi traditional literature. It is also a contribution to discourse analysis. While the texts given as examples are all well-formed and typical, no explicit apparatus or theory is considered for the purposes of evaluation. Such an effort would take, minimally, the expertise of a native Hopi-speaking coauthor. Although the possibility of articulating a Hopi esthetic theory of literature (including song-poems and therefore music) is intriguing, it is beyond the scope of the present work.

Comparisons between Hopi and other Pueblo literatures is minimal in this work, because there is simply no comparable treatment of them. The two exceptions are Zuni narrative and Pueblo music (with a small body of research). I have however included an extensive comparison of Hopi with other songpoem styles, because there is sufficient information for such an analysis. I have refrained from comparing in detail Dennis Tedlock's work on traditional Zuni narrative with my own work on Hopi traditional narratives, preferring to defer discussion until a truly pan-Pueblo narratology is possible.

Attention has been paid, however, to researchers working in ethnopoetics (Hymes, Tedlock, Sherzer, Woodbury, and others) and in performance
theory (Bauman, and others), because of the current importance of these
two ways of looking at Native American and other oral literatures.
Discussing Hopi traditional literature in terms of ethnopoetics and performance has enriched the structural, discourse analysis of the genres that
is the basis of the book. While it is tempting to compare the Hopi data
with comparable genres in other Native American traditions, I have
refrained from such an undertaking, again because the necessary literature is unavailable. Indeed, the present work is a pioneering effort, being
the only structural survey of the main genres of a single tradition north
of the Meso-American culture area to date.

It is my hope that this work will stimulate similar efforts in the American
Southwest and elsewhere, and that eventually studies of Native American
literature may make significant contributions to the field of comparative
literature. In writing this work, I am especially grateful to my teacher Emory
Sekaquaptewa and his family, who made possible my Hopi education. I
owe a great debt of thanks as well to the many Hopi people who have
helped sympathetic outsiders to understand the rich, publicly oriented
parts of their changing, living culture, as well as the outside persons who
worked with them. The assistance of an anonymous reviewer for the
University of New Mexico Press is gratefully acknowledged, and I owe
special thanks to my parents, my cousin Donald Grams, Loretta Jewell,
and Daphne Scott, all of whom assisted in the final redaction of this book.
Daphne Scott, Ana Alonso, and Ted Coyle read revisions of earlier drafts.
Beth Hadas, Liz Varnadoe, and David Margolin of the University of New
Mexico Press have also been very helpful with the project. Ken Hill and
Emory Sekaquaptewa helped in checking the Hopi texts. Thanks also to
Bethel College for permission to use Hopi materials from that institu-
tion's H. R. Voth collection, to the University of Chicago Press for per-
mission to use "Coyote and Wren," and to the Hopi Cultural
Preservation Office and Emory Sekaquaptewa for permission to reprint
his eloquent address on the use of the Hopi language.

HOPI HAS SIX DIFFERENT vowel sounds. All but one of these has an approximation in English. The Hopi alphabet has only one letter or combination of letters for each sound, unlike the spelling system for English. The five vowels that are similar to vowels in English are the following:

a	as in	father
e		met
i		machine
o		wrote
u		put

Each of these five vowels has only the value that it has in the English key word. Try pronouncing the following Hopi words—the consonants in these words are as in English:

pas	very
pep	there
sihu	flower
momi	toward the fore
tuwa	found

In English, it is possible to have long vowels; these simply last longer than the "short" versions of the vowel. Compare the vowels in italic in the English key words below:

father	far
met	meddle
street	machine
wrote	lode
put	pudding

In Hopi, there are long vowels just as in English. These are written by doubling the vowel.

paas	carefully
peep	almost
siihu	intestines
moomi	pigeon-toed
tuuwa	sand

If you compare the meanings of the two sets of Hopi words given thus far, you will discover that vowel length is important in Hopi.

Before introducing the sixth Hopi vowel, it is important to learn about the consonant *q*. Compare the two following English words:

key
coal

Both begin with a "k"; the one in *key* is made with the tongue further forward than the "k" in *coal*. This is the difference between the Hopi letter *k* (as in *key*) and the Hopi letter *q* (the *c* in *coal*).

kita	say
qala	forehead

It happens to be the case that the Hopi letter *q* occurs only before the following vowels in native words: *a*, *ö*, and sometimes *e*.

Hopi has a sixth vowel not found in modern English. It is written as an "o" with two dots over it (ö). It is made by saying the *e* in m*e*t while rounding the lips. The tongue and jaw stay the same as for m*e*t; only the lips move. Hopi *ö* is similar to the *u* in the English word p*u*rple.

qötö	head
qöötö	suds

As you can see, there is a long *öö* and a short *ö*, as with the other Hopi vowels.

The following consonants are pronounced approximately as in English.

h	as in	hat
k		skate
1		long
m		man
n		no
p		spot
t		state
w		wool
y		yes

These require no special comment, but note that *k*, *p*, and *t* do not have a puff of air after them (just as there is no puff of air after English *k*, *p*, *t* after the letter s: compare *sk*ate with *K*ate.

In Hopi, some consonants are written as **digraphs** (combinations of two letters), just as some consonants are in English (examples: *ch*urch, *sh*ip, etc.). The following are the Hopi consonants that are written with more than one letter.

kw	qu	as in	question
ky	cu		cue
ng	ng		sing
ngw	ng w		sing well
ngy	ng y		sing your best
ts	ts		cats

There are three other consonants in Hopi that an English speaker can produce with relative ease.

r	as in	measure
v		Spanish Havana
'		uh-oh

The Hopi *r* is produced by curling the tip of the tongue against the roof of the mouth and then vibrating. The Hopi *v* is made by vibrating both lips together. The glottal stop is made by momentarily stopping the airflow through the throat.

Hopi has combinations of vowels, just as English does. The second member of a Hopi vowel cluster is always either *w* or *y*.

aw	ow	as in	cow
ay	ie		pie
ew	e + w		met + w
ey	ai		bait
iw	ew		new
iy	ey		key
ow	(doesn't occur)		
oy	oy		toy
öw	u	as in purple + w	
öy	u	as in purple + y	
uw	u	as in put + w	
uy	u	as in put + y	

Consider the vowels in italic in the following English sentences.

I look at them.
I look at thèm!
We do it.
Don't dò it!

Notice that your voice drops a little in pitch in the second of each pair. This is called **falling tone**, and it is written with a slanting accent mark over the vowel. In English, falling tone is used to indicate a command.

In the Third Mesa (Oraibi) dialect of Hopi, falling tone is used to indicate different words. It only occurs with long vowels and vowel clusters.

aasi	wash someone's hair
àasi	sneeze
kweetsi	flung aside
kwèetsi	scurry
wiiki	take them
wìiki	catch up
poosi	eye/seed

pòosi	fall down
tsööqö	lame
tsôöqö	fastened upright
uu'uyi	planting
ùu'uyi	your plant

The letter ô indicates a falling tone on the vowel ö.

INTRODUCTION

THIS BOOK IS ABOUT the main **genres** of Hopi literature. The structure of the major public forms of Hopi traditional discourse will be considered, with some discussion of smaller or related types. The indigenously named genres include narratives (*tuutuwutsi*), direct address forms (*tsa'alawu*, "public announcing"; related discourse varieties include oration, prayer, and conversation), songs (*taawi*), and songpoems (*tawlawu*, "singing"). The problems involved in constructing such a native typology include: distinguishing subgenres of narrative, accommodating personal narratives, relating different direct address practices, and considering the short folkloric genres (sayings, proverbs) that are rarely reported for Native American groups. The present treatment will address these issues to some extent, but the main thrust is to lay an analytic foundation by considering the mechanics of each main type of Hopi literature.

TABLE I. HOPI TRADITIONAL LITERARY GENRES

stories (*tuuwutsi*), including coyote stories (*istutuwutsi*)

announcements (*tsa'alawu*)
    ritual (*wimtsa'alawu*)
    secular (*qa wimtsa'alawu*)

prayers (*unangwvàasi*)

formulaic expressions/admonishments

oration

6

ritual speech (*wimlavayi*)
speech (*lavay'oyi*)

song (*taawi*)
    songs
        lullabies (*puwati/puwvitstawi/titaptawi*)
        children's game songs (*tsakotawi*)
        story songs (*tuwutstawi*)
        gambling songs (*sosokwtawi*)
        grinding songs (*ngumantawi*)

    songpoem (*yewatawi*)
        kachina songs (*katsintawi*)

This study considers the structural characteristics of each genre recognized by Hopis and relates them to contextual and cultural factors. Central to this approach is the analysis of actual examples presented in bilingual format.

Each named category is characterized by obligatory **genre signatures** and a number of optional typifying features, as well as by a distinctive distribution of information. Another dimension of difference involves content: some genres have a high proportion of stock or formulaic material and are relatively closed, while a higher degree of interaction between performer and audience may lead to more variable content. In oral narratives or jokes, verbal interaction between performer and audience is expected and even required. In direct address genres, indirect feedback may be present, but the performer's voice predominates. In poetry or songs, the text world is completely closed; there is no interaction between performer and audience. Varying degrees of interaction, then, along with expected differences in semantic and emotive content, are the parameters that shape Hopi literature. In addition, the **validation** of a performance (its acceptance and appreciation by the audience) relies to some extent on predictable aspects of structure, which will also be discussed in the course of this study.

Hopi traditional narratives are divided into sections that are defined by reference to relative proximity: the opposition of nearness ("this," "here") as opposed to distance ("that," "there") is used to distinguish between first mention of **topics** and subsequent mention within the same section. A section is made up of **lines**; a line is usually a single sentence in length.

Lines are the important structural units below the section level. Each section embodies a series of narrative functions (Setting, Desire, Plan, Journey, Realization) that metaphorically casts every story as a journey. Each of these journey functions is realized by one or more formally marked subsections (one function per subsection, a function in several subsections, rarely several functions in a single subsection).

One genre signature, the **quotative particle** *yaw* ("it is said/they say"), occurs in nearly every narrative line and is always excluded from the quoted speech of characters. Lower level architecture may be of several sorts: local (subsection internal) "topic chains" may be defined by special suffixes, and a single line may be highlighted by deviations from the rigid SOV (Subject, Object, Verb) word order of Hopi, by successive subordinate clauses, and by occasional parallelism in wording or syntax. Often a series of subordinated clauses will form a quatrain that is rhetorically significant. Hopi narrative versification is predictable to some extent, just like other aspects of Hopi narrative practice.

The appropriateness of this model of Hopi traditional narratives is underscored by the fact that their constituent formalism has survived editing into an alien format (published as Western prose), that they have been used to validate and shape biblical stories as genuine narratives, and that the formalism has endured unchanged amid the rapid changes that have permeated Hopi life since 1945. Moreover, this structural model describes stories edited from the performances of different Third Mesa storytellers as well as stories from outside Third Mesa, but it does not fit the summaries of stories written in Hopi by a non-Hopi (Voth).

Further corroboration of this model comes from analyses of actual Hopi narrative performances. Their syntactic and lexical cues dovetail neatly with the prosodic cues that define lines (intonation and pausing). When the syntactic and prosodic cues do not coincide, there is always verbal feedback from the audience. The audience always responds verbally at the beginning of each new section, and most such response from the audience is preceded by increased volume and pitch on the part of the performer. The formal means of segmenting, structuring, and highlighting a story not only guarantees that the performance is a bona fide example of Hopi narration, but actually facilitates all of the evaluative interaction between narrator and audience.

Hopi direct address genres use many of the same discursive practices as traditional narratives: **deictic** ("pointing") marking of sections in longer examples, use of **proximals** (such as "here" and "this") for marking discourse topics, chains of subordinate clauses (especially when grouped into quatrains), definition of lines by both syntactic and prosodic means, and the use of syntactic-prosodic mismatch as a means of highlighting. What distinguishes "announcing" from narration is the combination of **indirection** (indefinites such as "someone" and modals such as "perhaps") and lack of audience response as a genre signature. Indirection refers to the avoidance of direct address by several means, chief of which is the use of indefinite pronouns instead of second person pronouns. Unlike public announcements (*tsa'alawu*), which are further distinguished by various peculiarities (the Rise-Hold-Fall intonation pattern, use of the quotative *yaw*, emphatic *-y*, the introducer *yaahahà*), orations and public prayers are typified only by indirection without immediate verbal response. Minimal direct address forms (proverbs, sayings, and perhaps certain fixed phatic expressions that function mostly for greeting and leave-taking) are primarily characterized by their brevity and conventionality (the exception being proverbs, which in addition always use indefinite pronouns and admonish by being cast as a negative command). Longer examples of announcements, public prayers, and orations all have the same structural features that elicit audience response in traditional narratives (marked ends of sections, syntactic-prosodic disjunction, sustained highlighting with increased volume and pitch), but these same cues elicit no such response in direct address types. This suggests that direct address form a single genre, distinct from traditional narrative and polite conversation (which uses indirection *with* response).

Hopi songs and songpoems are distinguished from other genres by singing vocalization and (almost always) **vocables** (syllables with emotive rather than semantic meaning); these features may be considered the signatures of the genre of "singing." In addition, **deictic sectioning** is absent from "singing," and none of the devices common to traditional narrative and direct address genres are exploited in songpoems and songs.

Hopi songs are either ritual or folkloric. Both types are fixed in both core musical structure and text, with folkloric songs having variation. Ritual songs are esoteric, used in kiva ceremonies when a particular religious society is in session, and have very minimal texts, the meaning of which is apparent only to initiates of the society and members of the clan that controls the society. Folkloric songs are acquired in a more or less fixed form (the folkloric core) in the course of some activity: game songs are learned by children playing games, gambling songs at gambling parties, lullabies around the women who are caring for the infants of a household, and story songs (*contes fables*) in the context of a particular story.

While songs appear to form a fixed body of literature, the genre of songpoems is infinite; Hopis continue to create new songpoems every year for public performances. Each songpoem is part of a series composed for a particular event and consists of a musical matrix containing a text. The form of a songpoem is AABBA, where A and B are major musical parts; the B sections are musically the most complex, while the accompanying text is the least variable semantically. This music-text relationship is thus a genre signature for songpoems.

The ethnoesthetics of the Hopis and other Pueblo Indians (Keresans, Zunis, and Tewas) includes a native terminology for the parts of the songpoem and for describing performance practice. Songs and songpoems in Hopi culture are usually performed in some communal activity, which brings up once again the degree of interaction between performer(s) and audience. With narratives, the text world of the story is invaded by ritualized verbal feedback from the audience. The narrator, moreover, may give asides and metacomments, so that a traditional Hopi narrative is much more than the pruned, edited story of Western prose fiction. This formalized interaction in actual narrative performances is predictable to a great extent: the audience responds to a combination of syntactic and prosodic cues.

The same structuring devices are also used in longer instances of the direct address genres (such as orations), but there is no audience response expected. Direct address is traditionally marked in Hopi culture by a principle of indirection, whether in conversation or in formal direct address (announcements, orations, public prayers). Traditional narratives are more "open" than direct address in a public context, because they allow verbal interaction between participants. Direct address genres are more "closed" in this sense, and songs and songpoems are completely "closed"; they exist unto themselves and share none of the structuring devices found in other genres. On the level of performance, then, a theory of Hopi literature may be predicated on the quality of expected interaction between performer(s) and audience.

◊

Having outlined the plan of the book, and reported the main characteristics of Hopi traditional genres, it remains to sketch a background of the culture in which Hopi traditional genres are situated. What follows is obviously not a complete ethnography or even a bibliographic guide to the main sources. It is an orientation to introduce the uninformed reader to the broader outline of Hopi culture.

The culture of the Hopi Indians, one of the most studied and famous of native North American peoples, is a Pueblo culture (see the bibliographic note at the end of this Introduction). The Spanish called these peoples "Town" (Pueblo) Indians because they lived in agricultural villages with masonry buildings. For at least a thousand years, the Hopis have lived in northern Arizona, depending on dry farming, hunting, and after the arrival of the Spanish, herding cattle and sheep. Wage work and sales of art (pottery, weaving, basketry, jewelry, kachina dolls) augment their contemporary economy. Service industries, retailing, and government employment are also important in the reservation economy.

Some of the existing eleven villages are headed by a hereditary village chief, and about half are governed by elected councils. Since the 1950s, the U.S. government has dealt with the Hopis through a Hopi Tribal Council, which follows a constitution dating from the 1930s (a product of the "Indian New Deal"). By the 1990s, nearly all of the villages elected and sent their allotted representatives.

The Hopis reckon a person's descent matrilineally, and one belongs to one's mother's clan. Individuals must marry outside their own clan (and ideally that of their father). A hereditary chief must come from the clan that founded the village. Ceremonies are "owned" by different clans, though persons outside the clan are admitted to membership in each clan-governed cult. In this way, the village is ceremonially integrated; at the same time, sacred knowledge is spread in such a way that no single individual knows everything. In the 1800s, there was a major ceremonial activity nearly every lunar month.

The kachina cult, which inspires much of Hopi traditional art, is famous for its masked dancing and kachina doll representatives. Kachinas are perfect beings, some of which may be anonymously ancestral, that visit the villages during the growing season and give kachina dolls to uninitiated girls and sometimes other females. Between the ages of about six and eleven, every Hopi child is initiated into the kachina cult. After initiation, each male may make kachina dolls and participate in the kachina dance dramas.

Hopis believe that everything progresses toward good; evil is eventually rewarded with nonexistence. The word *Hopi* means "of positive attitude," and this is shown by appropriate behavior. Anxiety and other negative emotions will be manifested as disease and bad luck. The public aspects of ceremonies create a collective positive feeling that is believed to attract rain, prosperity, health, and longevity to the community.

The Hopi language is a member of the Uto-Aztecan language family, which also contains (among others): Comanche, Shoshone, Ute, Piman, Yaqui, and Nahuatl. Within this language family, however, Hopi has no close relatives. There are four dialects of Hopi: the dialect of Third Mesa, the variety of the majority of the population (spoken in the villages of Oraibi, Hotevilla, Bacavi, Upper and Lower Moencopi, and Kykotsmovi); the dialect of Shongopavi (also spoken in Shipaulavi); the dialect of Mishongnovi; and First Mesa (spoken in Walpi and Sichomovi). The other Pueblo languages, all spoken in New Mexico except for Arizona Tewa, are completely unrelated to Hopi. See Pronouncing Hopi (p. 1) and the Sketch of Hopi Grammar (p. 207) in this volume.

One of the villages on First Mesa (Hano) has traditionally been bilingual in First Mesa Hopi and Arizona Tewa. This latter language was originally spoken in the Galisteo Basin near Santa Fe in New Mexico. In the late 1690s, the Tewas from that area left to escape the domination of Spanish culture after the reconquest following the great Pueblo Revolt of 1680. According to the Hopis, these people sought refuge at Hopi. Arizona Tewa is distinct from Rio Grande Tewa, which is spoken in six villages north of Santa Fe, although speakers of each variety can understand one another with some difficulty.

The modern Pueblo cultures can be traced to the Basketmaker culture (ca. 100 B.C. to ca. A.D. 400), known through archaeological remains. Branches of this culture developed in northern Arizona and northern to central New Mexico, southern Utah, and southwestern Colorado. Known by archaeologists as Pueblo peoples after masonry housing became prevalent (ca. A.D 700–900), they are popularly called the Anasazi, an anglicized form of the Navajo word for "enemy ancestors." This word is offensive to Pueblo peoples, who rely on their own terms for their ancestors (the Hopi term is *Hisatsinom*, "Ancient People").

Over the course of time, the Pueblo peoples, including the Hopis, developed a way of life based on small village communities of from 250 to perhaps 1200 persons. The agricultural triplex of corn, beans, and squash (supplying the amino acid equivalent of meat when eaten together) provided the basis of settled life, although hunting traditionally accounted for about half of the estimated protein intake. In addition to masonry buildings, the pit houses of Basketmaker times survived as kivas, ceremonial structures that also served as men's clubs. Basketry, ceramics, textiles, carving, and painting developed into sophisticated art by the fourteenth century, and the performing arts (music, poetry, and dance-drama) and verbal arts (narratives and orations) of the Hopis and other Pueblo peoples, though untraceable, undoubtedly developed complexity at the same time.

Around A.D. 1250, a severe drought affected much of the American Southwest. Communities gathered into large villages of about a thousand people, which were located in defensible positions on hills some distance from the low-lying fields. Warfare appears to have intensified, and the first material evidence of the kachina cult appears. Pueblo territory shrank to roughly the area the groups occupy today.

Spanish expeditions between 1539 and 1542 brought the Pueblo Indians into contact with European culture for the first time. They were not impressed, and the Spaniards, finding no gold or other "precious" substances, left them alone until 1598, when a Spanish colony was established in New Mexico. By the 1630s, there were Christian mission churches in all of the larger Pueblo villages, including those of the Hopis. Contact was intense and initially cooperative; for example, there were choirs, entire orchestras, and even pipe organs at several churches in New Mexico by the 1650s, with trained music teachers for the Indians. The details of Spanish-Pueblo rapprochement vanished in the near complete destruction of Spanish culture and records in the Pueblo Revolt of August 1680, which was brought on by overtaxation and intolerance of Indian religions.

By 1693, the Spanish were back, but they never recovered the Hopi area. During the 1700s and 1800s, the Hopis were plagued by drought and the warlike habits of their Navajo and Ute neighbors. The contributions of the Spanish became traditional in Hopi culture during this period: livestock (the horse for transportation, cattle and sheep replacing game animals), wool replacing the traditional cotton, some cultivated plants (mostly fruit trees), and metal technology. Anglo-American culture made the most impact on Hopi culture after World War II. The legacy of the Americans has been the first sustained pan-Hopi government, adoption of a money economy, a questioning and redefining of Hopi identity (largely because of education and mass media), and improved health conditions.

Hopi activities fit into a calendar round of lunar months. The year is divided into two halves: the cold season and the growing season. In the cold season, men hunt and work a wide variety of textiles, while women continue the culinary arts, child rearing, collecting work (firewood and water), and crafts that they engage in all year. In the warm season, men farm and work at the kachina cult.

Winter is traditionally the time for storytelling and, formerly, gambling. Raconteurs may be male or female. Since the growing season is also the kachina season, kachina songpoems are composed, rehearsed, and performed during this time. At either end of the growing season the social dances take place (Buffalo in January, Butterfly in July or August), with their own distinctive songpoem forms. Active participants in the kachina dance-dramas are initiated males, while participants in the social dances are both male and female. The composers of songpoems are all male.

Public direct address genres (chants/announcements, orations, public prayer) are used throughout the year, and the performers are male (though they may speak for anyone in the village). Other direct address genres (prayers, admonitions, sayings) are appropriately used by both female and male speakers throughout the year (and not typically in public).

The many details of the bulk of the Hopi ethnographic literature (but not its appropriate interpretation) may be accessed through the definitive bibliography of Laird (1977), which covers materials to 1975. Useful summaries of Hopi and other Pueblo cultures may be found in Dozier (1970) and Ortiz (1979). Some works of particular interest to general readers are the ethnography of Titiev (1944), the ethnography of Thompson and Joseph (1944), the mythography of Courlander (1971), and the histories of James (1974) and Whiteley (1988).

The cultural context, value, and performance dynamics of traditional narratives, direct address genres, and songpoems will be taken up in the relevant chapters.

Part 1

HOPI TRADITIONAL NARRATIVES

THE TRADITIONALLY APPROPRIATE TIME for storytelling is *Kyaamuyaw*, a lunar month between December and January, also called *Tuwutsmuyaw*, "Story Month." As is true in much of the American Southwest, summer is the least appropriate time for storytelling, since,

> Hak taala' tuutuwutsqw hakiy tsuu'a kuukingwu.
> If one tells stories in the summer, then a rattlesnake will bite them.

The storytelling season is also that of the winter solstice (*Soyalangwu*), which has many esoteric religious implications and requires more than usual quietude and inactivity, especially at night. Most traditional storytelling takes place at night, providing an occasion for family gatherings and also for visiting friends. Narrators may be male or female. Sometimes each adult present tells a story in turn, in a *tuwutsqöniwma*, "story circle."

The content of narratives varies widely, including coyote stories and other fables; legends and historical tradition (*i' hapi pas qa yaw'i, pas antsa*, "this is not hearsay, it's real/true"); tales told for sheer entertainment (including themes usually avoided in real life, such as death, ghosts, and sorcery); and secular forms of myths (as I am glossing certain of the Hopi traditional narratives). Narrative performance practices require that members of the audience respond at certain carefully marked structural and dramatic junctures, as discussed in chapter 3.

〽

The major means of structuring Hopi narrative discourse (narratives and longer orations and announcements) into sections is the use of **spatial deixis** in the form of a binary opposition involving relative proximity: nearness (**proximal reference**) as opposed to distance (**distal reference**). Hopi indicates several degrees of spatial distance:

neutral	ep	'at the place'
proximal	yep	'here'
distal	pep	'there'
hyperdistal	ayám	'yonder'

When the main actors or props in a story are first mentioned, they are surrounded with indications of nearness, such as 'this' or 'this way.' Elements set off in this way are called **discourse topics**, since they are important throughout the discourse or a major part of it. On subsequent mention within a section of a story, the discourse topics established at the beginning of the section are marked with distal references, such as 'that' or 'that way.' Because they are semantically indicated, the mechanics of Hopi section marking survive the transcription and editing of taped performances into the alien format of Western prose. They were also used in the Hopi translation of the New Testament in the longer narratives, irrespective of prescribed narrative boundaries (biblical chapter and verse boundaries).

Equally important for sectioning is a basic narrative thematic sequence to which all traditional Hopi narratives conform. I will refer to this sequence, a journey metaphor, as the Hopi **narrative schema**. Remarkably, every story is cast as a journey away from the home base(s) of the protagonist(s).

Storyworthiness is another factor involved in Hopi narratives, and it is pragmatically indicated in a somewhat different manner from the narrative highlighting used in Western narratives. In the latter, **evaluative devices** such as use of the word *very*, repetition, interjections, and expressive phonology are used to establish the validity of a spoken narrative. Hopi traditional narratives differ in largely lacking an **evaluation section** (Shaul et al. 1987) that highlights the purpose or motivation, in contrast to the personal narratives in American culture studied by Labov and Waletsky (1967) and Western prose fiction studied by Pratt (1977).

There remains one final major structural feature of Hopi traditional stories to be noted. As in the traditional narrative practices of some other Native American cultures, a quotative expression is used as a genre signature. Thus,

Kroskrity (1985, 1993:143–75) has shown that the quotative particle *ba* in Arizona Tewa traditional narratives is in significant complementary distribution with its absence: a quotative appears in all **narrative clauses** (in which a character does not speak), but never in **quotation clauses** (those involving direct speech of characters). In exactly the same way, the Hopi quotative *yaw*, 'it is said/they say,' is used to create a narrative fabric (Wiget 1987:329). The consistent use of the quotative as a genre signature for narrative, as well as the consistent use of spatial deixis to define sections, also survived the translation of Hopi traditional narratives into the prose style of Western fiction.

Because of the richness of oral performance, some researchers believe that texts without sound recording cannot or should not be used to analyze narrative organization. The preservation in such **flat texts** of features diacritical in Hopi narrative organization shows that this notion is false and in fact provides convincing evidence for the "particle" approach. Moreover, this approach has implications for narrative processing, discussed in chapter 3.

1

THE HOPI NARRATIVE SCHEMA

SHAUL (1987a) FOUND THE FOLLOWING underlying schema for Hopi narratives, both coyote stories and other genre types:

Setting — Desire — (Plan) — Journey — Realization.

The design of a well-formed Hopi narrative involves at least one journey away from a home base. The plan and journey functions may be realized by the same section(s).

Hopi traditional narratives available in published form (Malotki 1978; Lomatuwa'yma, Lomatuwa'yma, and Namingha 1994; Lomatuwa'yma, Lomatuwa'yma, Namingha, et al. 1995; Malotki and Lomatuwa'yma 1984, 1985, 1987a, 1987b, 1987c; some materials in Geertz and Lomatuwa'yma 1987) are all flat texts, such as those used by Hymes in much of his work. All of these published narratives consist of sections defined by spatial deixis that follow the Hopi narrative schema. New information is marked with proximal deictics, such as 'this' or 'here,' while old information (subsequent mention within a section) of established actors or prop entities is marked with distal deictics, such as 'that' or 'there.' There may also be a clustering of proximals at the end of a section. In the example below, from the beginning of a coyote story episode, the first mention of the topic 'clouds' is coded with proximals (*ima*, 'these,' *yepeq*, 'hereabouts'). Subsequent mention of the clouds within the section involves distal deictics (*puma*, 'those,' objective case form *pumuy*; and *pangsoq*, 'along there'). Proximals are indicated by capital letters, and distals appear in italic in both the original and the translation. Please note that texts are presented in **lines**, usually a single sentence in length. This is a departure from all previous representation of Hopi narrative texts.

Yaw IMA oo'omawt YEPEQ Öngtupqawveq ki'yyungwa . . .
Pay kya as pam *pangsoq*nen paalayamuy *pumuy* amumi paalayamuy
oovi tuuvingtaqw
Pay kya yaw as *puma* naanakwhe' angqw yoknawisni.
(Malotki and Lomatuwa'yma 1985:106)

¶

They say THESE clouds OVER HERE were living at the Grand
Canyon . . .
Maybe if he went *there* to ask *those ones* for their juice,
Then just maybe yaw *those ones* would assent and (come) from *along*
there to make it rain.

In the translation (which is mine, not the editors'), the initial mention of 'clouds' and their location is marked with proximals; the next mention is one clause away, and both receive distal marking. The same method of sectioning stories is used in all the stories published by Malotki and Lomatuwa'yma. The next example (Malotki and Lomatuwa'yma 1984:151) illustrates the range of deictic markers that may occur; proximals and distals are indicated as before.

"pay pi son I' nuy angwu'ytanikyangoy,"
yaw YAN wuuwa.
"pay nu' IT pas sowe'
pu' nu' kawayvasayat pas himu'yvaniy,"
yaw YAN wuuwa.
"nu' IT himu'yvaqw
pàasat pu' itam son tsöngmokiwyungwmantani,
pas itam pas ITsa akw yesniy."
yaw YAN wuuwaqe
pu' yaw pay *pam* matsaakwat suymoyta.

¶

"THIS guy shouldn't get the best of me,"

she thought THIS WAY.
"If I just devour THIS ONE,
then the melon field will be mine."
she thought THIS WAY,
"I'll own THIS (field).
and then we won't be hungry from here on out,
we'll just subsist on THIS."
So thinking THIS WAY,
she quickly mouthed *that* horned toad.

The proximal marking correlates with the female coyote's anxiety as revealed in the internal monologue. The sudden shift of attention to the victim (a horned lizard) is marked with distal deixis; the horned toad has already been established within the section.

It is instructive at this point to provide an example of the fit between formally defined sections and the Hopi narrative schema: the use of deixis to section a Hopi traditional narrative into units that constitute a journey (table 1.1). Sections are marked with Roman numerals, and enough of each section is excerpted in translation to show how the section is established and to reveal its content. Each excerpt in table 1.1 is the beginning of a proximally defined section.

TABLE 1.1. SECTIONAL ANALYSIS OF A HOPI COYOTE STORY[A]

	THIS Coyote lived at Coyote Gap
	hunting, *that* was his only know-how . . .
	[he finds a nest of crows on the cliff slope]
II	"if I get 'em, I'll roast 'em, and really chow down,"
	THIS he thought;
	[he goes for help, killing a rabbit on the way]
	but refrained THIS WAY from eating it . . .
	that doing, he went outside his house
	[to summon other coyotes]
III	THIS WAY, more or less he called,
	THIS doing, a coyote arrived from the north;
	[he explains situation] . . .
IV	when they had done THIS [form a chain],

[they find they can't reach; they continue
to recruit till there are five] . . .

V   [they had closed their eyes to avoid being dizzy]:
the one behind the lead coyote thinks LIKE THIS:
"maybe if I open my eyes, I can see what he's doing;
"I won't get dizzy" . . .
that doing, [he sees the lead coyote shit while
straining;
he laughs, dropping the bottom coyote] . . .

VI   the next above thinks LIKE THIS: . . .
so THIS NEXT ONE above opens his eyes;
[repeat process, all the way to the first Coyote] . . .

VII   [the first Coyote opens his eyes]:
THIS made him do the same thing:
. . . *doing that*, [the other one remaining falls;
Coyote laughs so hard, he loses his own grip] . . .

VIII   THIS is how the coyotes fared;
THIS DOING, they didn't eat crow:
and nobody got any roast rabbit.
It ends THIS WAY.

a.   "Ii'ist Naahahayya: The Coyote Chain" (Malotki and Lomatuwa'yma
1984:150–59).

b.   First mention (without proximal marking) of a main character in the first
section serves to establish that entity as new information. (The mention of
a name, such as Coyote, has the force of proximal marking.)

c.   The translation is mine.

The sections of this narrative cohere to the journey metaphor (Setting-Desire-(Plan)-Journey-Realization). The setting (section I) is directly followed by a strong desire on the part of Coyote (II), when he sees a nest of crows on a cliff as he is out hunting. The journey and plan functions are combined in an iterated series of sections (III, IV); Coyote goes to recruit fellow coyotes from each direction to form a coyote chain to get down and pilfer the nest. The resolution is also a series of sections (V, VI, VII): the coyote on the bottom strains so hard that he shits, which causes the coyote above to laugh and release his tail, dropping him. This chain (III-IV) and chain reaction (V-VI-VII) are iconic; not only is the

21

deictic marking mechanically useful in the story, but the design it creates functions rhetorically as well.

There are several ways in which Hopi traditional narratives are structured below the section level. The use of various specifiers to create **local topic chains** (topics highlighted only momentarily or within a section, not a discourse topic) is one of the main devices used. Hopi traditional narratives are versified in a way similar to the ethnopoetic analyses of Hymes (1981) and D. Tedlock (1983); Hopis share some aspects of **scansion** (criteria and application of rules to determine the lines and grouping of lines in a text) based on preferential syntactic subordination that groups lines into **quatrains** (groups of four lines, especially lines crucial to the plot), much as they share a common narrative schema and a common sectioning convention. Subsectional architecture (local topic chains, **versification** [the hierarchical organization of lines in a text or text section], devices that reinforce other primary markers) is important for the issue of evaluation. For example, certain specifiers (*-wa, -wat, -toyna*) are used to highlight topics that occur only within a section of discourse defined by spatial deixis (Shaul 1987b).

In the following abstracted section (Malotki 1978:44–45), the adverbial specifier *-wat* (something like English *-ly*, except that it applies to a context, not just a single word) creates a local topic chain. The ellipsis points indicating the deletion of narrative clauses indicate a distance of from one to ten clauses. Each *wa(t)* is marked with italic and bold face.

    pangqw pu' yaw puma kwiniwq***wat*** nakwsu . . .
        puma suukw kuktuwa . . . puma warikna . . .
        pay yaw qa wuuyavonit pay paki . . .
    "um kwiningqöyngaq***wat***, pu' nu' yang***wat***ni" . . .
    tupko'at kwiningqöyngaq***wat*** aqw tumotsoki'ykyangw . . .
    noq pangq***wat*** yaw iyoho'o . . .

                        ⌂

    from there these two set out *toward the north* . . .
    they found the tracks of one . . . made it run . . .
    not before long it entered under a rock . . .
    "you take *the northern side*, I'll take *along here*" . . .
    the younger brother sat down at the *northern side* . . .
    then, *along there*, he aimed his bow . . .
    now *along there* it was cold . . .

The local topic chain marked with *-wat* creates a scaffold for the entire narrative episode, which corresponds to the **plan function:**

towards the north — *wat₁*
the north side — *wat₁*   along here — *wat₂*
at the north side — *wat₁*
along there — *wat₁*
along there — *wat₁*

Thus, Hopi traditional narratives use some grammatical cues to distinguish levels of discourse below the section. This and other subsectional structuring devices (other specifiers, contrastive and focus constructions, versification by subordination, marked syntactic structures that reinforce section closures) may serve to create a feeling of authenticity. Along with the genre signature (the quotative *yaw*), Hopi traditional narratives employ **evaluative devices** to validate genre status at most levels (genre, section, various subsections).

Binarity in Hopi narrative provides for ease of processing, while helping to create storyworthiness by using cultural convention to shape the content of sections as episodes of a journey. Hopi has a range of spatial deictic possibilities (neutral, proximal, distal, hyperdistal [remote]), yet only two degrees of spatial reference are used in structuring discourse, much as binary contrasts are employed in other narrative traditions for ease of distinguishing clause and sentence levels (DuBois 1987). The model proposed here, along with the parallelism in line structure, provides a cognitive basis for identifying and savoring examples of a given genre. This approach is borne out in the corpus of published flat text narratives in Hopi, all of which are divided into sections defined by spatial deixis that conform to the schema proposed above.

Hopi traditional narratives all exhibit the same formal structure, and are all interactive. The audience, following the narrative schema, responds at appropriate points with *owi*, 'yes,' or *oo'*, 'yes,' or some other affirmation.

CORROBORATION OF HOPI NARRATIVE CONVENTIONS

Corroboration of the model proposed here of Hopi traditional narrative is possible by considering narrative conventions preserved in the earliest versions of narratives collected in the language (Voth ms.), which were recorded in haste and without regard for Hopi conventions, as well as in other Hopi narrative traditions and novel narratives in Bible translation.

VOTH'S THIRD MESA TEXTS

Henry R. Voth, while working as a missionary among the Third Mesa Hopis, collected many Hopi narratives. Very few, however, were collected in Hopi. In 1904, Qöyawayma, one of his Hopi colleagues, visited him in Newton, Kansas; many of the narratives in *Traditions of the Hopi* were dictated to Voth by Qöyawayma in Hopi, with Voth then dictating summaries in English to a stenographer. Some stories, however, he summarized in Hopi. Only one of Voth's summaries in Hopi is of substantial length (eight typescript pages, double-spaced); the others are one or two typescript pages.

The longer story ("Maskimiqw, A Journey to the Underworld") seems to have come from an actual performance of the myth, since it preserves the use of proximals to mark new mentions within a section of discourse. Kennard (1989) provides another version of this myth, in Second Mesa dialect. Voth's orthography has been retranscribed, so that long vowels are consistently shown and falling tone is marked; the same capitalization and italicization conventions are used as in the previous examples (see chapter 2 for significance of indentation).

MASKIMIQW

        Itàakiy ep Orayve yeesiwa.
        Pu' ayám Honletnömat kiyat ep yaw hak tiyo ki'yta
        Pam yaw ep tùmpoq
        nen aqw sutsep tsokiwta,
5   talavay.
        Niikyangw pam *put tuu'amit* sutsep aw wuuwanta.
        "Sen pas antsa yang hìitu yeese," pam wuuwanta.
        "Sen pas antsa hak mookye'
        "háqamningwu?" YAN wuuwanta.
10   "As himu nuy IMUY YANG aamiwyùngqamuy haqam yesqw
        "nuy aa'awnani."
        Pu' pam nuwu pay homngumnit ömàata.
        Pu' pàasat tùmpoq aqw'a.
        Pu' IT TAAWAT aw naawakna.
15   Pu' yaw aw pàngqawu,

"Ta'a,
"sen um YANG IMUY AAMIWYÙNGQAMUY sen
haqam yesqw
sen um tuwi'yta,"YAN yaw aw naawakna.
"Oovi um haqam tuwi'yte'
20   "nuy aa'awnani," YAN yaw naawaknat
pu' angqw nima,
pu' *pam* àapiy aqw *pàntsaki*,
aqw naawaknangwu.
Pu' *pam* naalös haqam aqw naawaknat
25   pu' aqw tsokiwta.
Noqw yaw angqaqw hak aw wuuvi.
Pam angqaqw wupqa pu' aw pàngqawu,
"Ta'a hinoq um nuy naawakna?"
"Owi," yaw kita *pam* tsokiwtaqa.
30   "Pay nu' sutsep IMUY YANG AAMIWYÙAMUY AMUMI
wuuwanta.
"Sen pas antsa hak ep suup qatsit ep qátungwu?"
Pu' yaw pàngqawu,
"Owí," yaw kita.
"Pay yeese.
35   "Sen pas um sùutaq'ewa
"amumi taatayniqa'e."
Pu' *pam tiyo* nakwha.
"Owí," yaw kita.
"Antsa," kita *pam Taawa*.
40   "Nu' ung tur IT máqani."
Pu' yaw hìita aw tavi.
"Ason um tapkiqw puwvaniqe
"pu' IT um hìisaq angqw sówani.
"Niikyangw ason ungu *pumuy* aa'awnani."
45 Antsa yaw kita tiyot aw'i.
"Nu' àapiyo," yaw kita Taawa.
Pu' yaw *pam tiyo* angqw nima,
kiy aw'i.
Pu' yaw ep pitu.
50 Pu' yaw yu'at noovalawu.
Pu' yaw puma nöönösaqw

pu' nay aw pàngqawu,
"Ina'a," yaw kita.
"Hay,
55   "pu' hímu'u?"
"Owí," yaw kita *pam tiyo.*
"Sen yaw antsa hak mookye'
"haqam qátungwu?
"Nu' tuwi'yvaniqey naawakna."
60   Pu' pàasat yu'at aw pàngqawu,
"Pay pi um qa *pantani*," yaw kita.
"Hal pay pi umuy."
"Owí," yaw kita *pam tiyo.*
"Owí nu' ason mihikqw puwve'
65   "sen nu qa iits taatayni," yaw kita.
"Ason oovi uma pas taawat yámakqe
"pas oovetiqw
"pu' uma inumi hintsani,
"pàasat sen nu' pítuni,
70   "taytani."
Pu' yaw na'at pàngqawu,
"Kur antsa'a," yaw kita.
Pu' yaw mihi.
Pu' yaw pam hìisaqw ngahuy angqw sowa.
75 Pàntit
yaw pam puwva.
Pay yaw pam pas mooki.
Pu' pam kur maskimiq'a.
Pu' Apòonive'e kur pam pitu.
80 Aqwhaqam a'ne' pöhu.
Aqw kwiningqöymiq haawi.
Noqw yaw ep haqam hak qatu.
Pay yaw *pam* hisat mooki.
"Noqw yaw *pami'i*," yaw tuwi'yta.
85 Pam yaw pàngqawu,
ep qátùuqa,
"Yaw um angqaqö?" yaw kita.
"Owí," *yaw pam tiyo* kita.
"Ta'a,

90   "um as nuy iikwìltani," yaw kita,
        pam ep qátùuqa.
        "Ngas'ew um naalös kwilakt
        "pep nuy távini."
     "Qa'é,
95   "nu' kyaktàyti," yaw aw kita *pam tiyo.*
        Pu' yaw *pam* àapiy'a.
        Pu' *pam* paqlawu,
        [pam] ep qátùuqa.
        Pu' pam àapiy hìisavoniqw
100   piw hak ep qatu.
        Pu' pay piw su'an aw lavàyti.
        Pu' yaw *pam* piw qa nakwha.
        Pu' yaw *pam* Awat'omi wuuvi.
     Noqw yaw angqaqw hak ahoyi.
105   Yaw hìita iikwìlta.
     Yaw hak wùuti kur qalavit hòota,
        niikyangw awatvosit ngat'a'yta.
        Niikyangw YANG qötötspuyat ang huur pakiwta.
        Pu' yaw pangqawu pam wùuti,
110   "Um nuy IT tavinani.
        "Qa'é" yaw kita pam tiyo.
        "Nu' kyaktàyti."
        Pu' *pam* àapiy piw'u.
        Pu' yaw aw pitu.
115   Piw hak angqö.
     Niikyangw pam yaw matat iikwiwta;
        niikyangw hömpawit ngat'a'yta.
        Pu' *putwakwat kukyat* yöngö aw somiwta,
        pu' suywakwat pöna.
120   Oovi kur pam hin kyaktayni.
     Hihin pavan kyaktàytiqö
        pam put a'ne söskwingwu.
        Pu' *pam* aw pàngqawu,
        "Um nuy IT tavinani!"
125   "Qa'é," yaw kita.
        "Nu' kyaktàyti."
        Pu' yaw *pam* piw àapiyo.

27

Àapiy pam a'ne wari.
Pu' yaw kur aqw pitu.
130   Noqw yaw ep haqam a'ne eyoyota.
Kur kwani'ytaqa.
Pam kwani'ytaqa aw pàngqawu,
"Um pitu," yaw aw kita.
"Owí," yaw pam tiyo kita.
135   Pu' yaw Kwani'ytaqa pàngqawu,
"Noqw um amumi taatayi?
"YAN um naawakna.
"Nu' oovi ung aa'awnani.
"Ep um aw mòoti pitu,
140   "*pam* hapi pas nukpana.
"Pam hapi talaa' yokvaniqw
"qa naawaknangwu.
"Pam hapi hìita hovaktuqat [akw] IMUY OO'MAWTUY AMUMI
hintsanqw
"*puma sòosoyam* watqangwu.
145   "Pu' piw ura sukw um aw pitu.
"Pam hakiy niinangwu.
"Pam hakiy qa lolomat aw panaqw
"put hak put akw mokngwu.
"Oovi puma kur hisat PEQW pítuni.
150   "Oovi puma naalös kwilakt
"pep qátungwu.
"Pu' IMA Awat'ove piw hòyta,
"iikwiwnuma,
"Puma piw pay naalös kwilakt
155   "pep qátungwu.
"Niikyangw puma nanalsikis pep qatut
"pu' àapiyningwu.
"Pay kur puma hisat PEQW ökini!
"Ta'a,
160   "yupá!
"Niikyangw um YANGWATNI.
"Pay pi ung aqw hàykyalaqw
"pu' ep haqam so'onqa eyoyotani."
Noqw antsa *pam* kur hàykyala[t],

165   noqw yaw eyoyota.
        Pu' antsa pam hakiy piw aw pitu.
        Pu' pay piw su'an aw lavàyti,
        "Um pitu?" yaw aw kita.
        "Owí," kita *pam tiyo.*
170   "Ta'a,
        "tumu," aw kita *pam kwani'ytaqa.*
        Pu' tiyot ngu'a,
           pu' àapiy ngu'yma.
        Puma pu' haqami hu'iyva.
175   Noqw yaw ep haqam qöhiwta.
        Pu' yaw *puma* aw pitu.
        Noqw pas a'ne hötsi,
        koysöt anta,
        niikyangw a'ne uwiwita.
180   "Ura um mòoti amumi pitu,
        "puma hapi PEW'I," kita.
        "Pumuy nu' PEQW qôönani.
        "Puma ep Orayve nunukpantu,
        "pumuy hapi PEQW nu' qööna.
185   "Pu' ngas'ew yámakni,
        "me' pam taqte'
        "kwitsve'
        "pu' yámakni;
          "pu' YANG ura ephaqam kwiitsingwu òopokiwtangwu.
190   "Pay *pan puma'a.*
        "Puma qa hìita noonova.
        "Puma qa haq hàalayya.
        "Pay pi naap unangwayniqö.
        "Ta'a,
195   "itam piw PEWNI."
        Pu' *puma* piw haqami hötsit aw pitu,
        aqwhaqam qa taala.
        "PEQW nu peetuy wahita.
        "Niikyangw puma pas sutsep tangawtangwu.
        "Pas puma qa haq nönga.
200   "Ta'a,
        "tuma'a,

"itam ahoyni.
"YAN piw um IT tuwi'yvaniqey naawakna."
Pu' put matavi.
205   Pu' *pam ayo'wat kwani'ytaqat* ahoy aw pitu.
Pu' yaw piw aw pàngqawu,
"Uma piw pitu?"
"Owi," yaw kita *pam tiyo.*
Pu' piw YANGWAT pöhu aw lalayi.
210   "YANGWAT um piw," kita.
Pu' antsa pam haqami kiimi pitu,
niikyangw mokiki.
Niikyangw pas qötsatsa ki'yyungwa.
Ep kiihut pas qalave kwani'ytaqa waynuma.
215   Pu' yaw pàngqawu,
"Um pitu?
"Ta'a,
"um PEWNI!"
Pu' yaw ngu'a,
220   pu' àapiy yaw kiimi yaw wiiki.
Pu' yaw aw pitu.
Piw yaw suukyawa mongwi kwani'ytaqa ep wunu,
pas kiy ep'e.
"Uma pitu?" amumi kita.
225   "Owi," *puma* naama kita.
Pu' yaw,
"Ta'a huvam páki'i!"
Pàasat yaw tuwat tiyot ngu'a,
pam kwani'ytaqa suukyawa.
230   Pu' paki.
Pu' antsa yaw hakim yeese.
Kur hakiy tuwi'yta.
Pam hisat Orayve as móngwiningwu.
Pu' yaw kwani'ytaqa aw pàngqawu,
235   put tiyot aw'i,
"YANTA,
"IT um tuwi'yvaniqey naawakna."
Noqw yaw pas wukosihut ep qatu,
pam mokqa mongwi.

240   Piw pàayom naanakwayngyapo
        sihut ang iniwyungwa mongvitu.
          "YANTA!" yaw kita pam kwani'ytaqa.
          "Pay IMA ep Orayve qa haq qa loloma,
            "sustep loloma.
245   "Paniqw puma YEP YANGYUNGWA.
          "Ta'a,
           "oovi itam YUK piw kuyvani."
          Pu' yaw piw paki.
      Pep yaw sòosoy himu tuusaqa piw uuyi,
250   pu' sishu hímu'u.
          "YANTAQAT oovi IMA ki'yyungwa," kita pam kwani'ytaqa.
          "YAN pi um naawakna.
          "Owí pas um ang taatayni.
          "Ta'a,
255 "um áhoyni!
      "Um tuu'awnani!
      "Me hak ep Orayve qa nukpanen,
        "so'on qa PEQW pítungwu.
      "Pay pi IMA NUNUKPANT so'on PEWYANI.
260   "Pay pi um aw taatayi!
      "Me,
        "pay *pep pöhu* amungem pasiwta.
      "Oovi um ep pite'
      "um IT YANTAQAT itàaqatsiy,
265   "um sòosok amumi lalavayni.
      "Noqw hak nengem ang hin wuuwankyangw
        "qátumantani.
      "YAN um naawakna;
        "um sòosok itàakiy aw pákìiqa'e
270   "um sòosok tuwi'yva;
            "niikyangw pay pi um hisat angkniqey unangwte'
            "pu' um ùungahuy um angqw hìisaqw sowani.
              "Niikyangw um IMUY unguy,
              "unay,
275   "puma IT AW lalavayni.
      "Noqw pas qa ephaqam *panyungngwu.*
      "Pay pi ilavayiy qa tuptsiwqa pay so'on YEP nùutum qatuni.

"Ta'a,
"yupá!
280 "Um pas wárikni!
"Taq ep ungu,
["unay],
"*puma* ung nùutayta."
Pu' yaw antsa *pam pangqw* a'ne wari.
285 Pu' kwanmongwit aw pitu ep,
pönalsive'e.
Pu' aw pàngqawu,
"Um pitu?" yaw kita.
"Owí," yaw kita pam tiyo.
290 "Kur antsa," yaw kita.
"Pay pi um a'ne wárikni!
"Taw ungu,
["unay],
"*puma* ung nùutayta."
295 Pu' pam angqw yuumosa piw a'ne warikiwta.
Pu' Awat'ove piw amumi pitu[qw]
ura *puma* ep sivilalwa,
puma pas u'uyingwutnìiqa'e.
Puma as Maskimiq
300 niikyangw pep naat sivilalwa.
Puma pep tsaawine'
paapu put uyangat qe'tini[qw]
pu' naap hisat Maskimi amumi pítuni.
Pu' pam amumi pítuqw
305 aw pangqawu pam ep qátùuqa,
"Ngaspi um àapiy piw áhoyi.
"Owí," kita pam tiyo.
Pàasat piw a'ne wárikiwta.
Pu' wùutit ep pitu.
310 Piw pam aw pàngqawu,
"Ngaspi um pay piw áhoyi."
"Owí," yaw kita.
Pàasat piw àapiy wárikiwta.
Pu' Apòonivi kwingningqöyve hakiy niinangwuqat aw pitu.
315 "Ngaspi um pay piw áhoyi," pàngqawu pam sivilàwqa.

32

"Owí," *pam* kita.
Panis kitat
pu' àapiy wari.
Pu' Apòonive hihin kwingingqöyve aw pitu.
320   Pu' yep ura *pam qa yoynawaknangwuqat* qatu.
Pam piw *pan* lavàyti.
"Owi," kita *pam tiyo*,
   pu' piw àapiy wari.
   Pu' kiy ep pitu,
325   Orayve'e.
     Pu' yaw qatungwuy aw paki.
     Pu' taawat yamakqw
pay pàasat taatayi.
     Pu' yaw *pam* qatuptu.
330   Qátuptuqe
yaw pep wuuwanlawu.
Taawa pay ooveti.
Pu' yu'at novayukùuqa'e
   pu' aw pòota.
335   "Um pay taatayi?" yaw kita pam yu'at.
"Owí," kita.
"Ta'a,
   "itam noonovani,
   "oovi um PEWNI," yu'at yaw kita.
340   Antsa pàngqawu *pam tiyo*.
Pu' *puma* noonova.
Yaw *puma* nöönösaqw
pàasat yaw na'at tuvingta *put tiyot*,
   "Hin um navota?" yaw kita.
345   "Owí," yaw kita,
   "Kur pas antsa yaw yeese," yaw kita.
"Antsa nu' sòosok epeq Maskiveq ang taatayi."
"Noq pey epeq mongwi YAN inumi lavàyti,
   "YAN nu' umuy aa'awnani.
350   "Kur pam kwanmongwi IMUY NUNUKPANTUY epeq qöqöna.
   "Pu' IMUY PEETUY kur qa taalat aqw piw wahita.
     "Pu' kur piw epeq IMA YEP momngwinitngwu
     "puma YEP lolomat yeese,

"pay kur *puma* piw epeq momngwitningwu.
355 "Pu' oovi nu' antsa epehaq YAN pumuy qatsiyamuy aw yori.
"Noqw pay oovi uma hisat nuy YEP qa taatayqw
"pay uma put ep qa pas hin wuuwantani.
"Pay kur pas yeese."
YAN yaw amumi lavàyti.
360 Pu' àapiy antsa *puma* naat sutsep yeese.
Pu' kur aqwniqey unàngwti.
Pu' yaw nay aw pàngqawu,
"Itana,
"itangu'u!"
365 "Hay," *puma* kita.
"Pay nu' piw ahoy aqwni," yaw kita.
"Ta'a," yaw kita *pam na'at.*
Pu' ep mihikqw *pam* put ngahu angk hìisaqw sowa.
Pu' yaw antsa pam puwva.
370 Nit pay yaw pam kur pas mooki.
Pu' yaw yumat tumoy'ytaniqa'e,
nösniqa'e
tiyot aw pòota.
Pay yaw kur mooki.
375 Pu' yaw *puma* nawus *put* mokyàata.
Pu' yaw *puma put* haqami ayóq Kuyvöt atpipo tavito.
Pep yaw oovi *puma put* aama.
Pu' àapiy *puma* pay yeese.
Noqw pu' *puma,*
380 na'at piw yu'at
put sölmoki,
tiyot.
Pu' yaw na'at pasmi'i.
Pu' yaw *pam* paasay ep pítùuqe
385 pu' paslawu.
Noqw YANG aqlaq himu wari.
Kur himu masa'ytaqa,
kur patro.
Pu' yaw aw lavàyti p*am patro,*
390 "Okiwa!" yaw kita.
"Okiw nuy ina sölmoki," kita nay aw'i.

34

Pu' yaw na'at pàngqawu,
"Owí!
"Nu' ung sölmoki."
395 "Pay pi um qa *pantani,*" yaw kita.
"Pay pi ura nu' umuy aa'awna.
"Ason naalötok nu' piw angqwni;
"oovi uma naama angqwni," kitat
pay àapiy waaya.
400 Pu' àapiy naalös tàlqw
pam na'at pàngqawu yuyat aw'i,
"Itam paapu naama awni," antsa yaw kita.
Pu' *pam nööma'at* nitkyata.
Pu' *puma* àapiy aw'i.
405 Pu' ep pituy.
Pu' yaw *puma* paslawu.
Pu' *pam kongya'at put nöömay aw* pangqawu,
"Pu' hapi hak pítuni," yaw kita.
"Yaw hak'i?" kita.
410 Naat YAN aw lalavayqw
pay kur pitu.
Antsa haqam amuqalap tötöqa.
Pu' antsa angqw amumi wari.
Pu' yaw amumi pitu.
415 Pay panis amumi pitut
pam yaw "Okiwa!" kita.
"Uma nuy sölmoki," kita.
Pu' yaw *pam* na'at pàngqawu,
"Owi!"
420 "Pay uma qa *pantani!*" yaw kita.
"Pay pi nu' kwangwaqtu."
Pu' yaw yu'at aw pangqawu,
"Owí,
"nu' umuy sölmokiwta!"
425 "Ta'a,
"*pay pi uma qa pantani!*" yuy aw kita.
"Pay nu' so'on umuy qa poptani."
Panis kitat
piw àapiy waaya.

430   Pu' yaw *puma* tapikiqw angqw nima.
       Pu' antsa àapiy na'at ep pasve waynumqw
       pam ep pítungwu.
       Àapiy yaw pay yeese.

▌

YÀASAVA!
Into the World of the Dead
       They were living at our village of Oraibi.
          Over at the place at Honletsnöma's house there lived a boy.
       That one at the edge of the mesa
          was always perched at the place
5   in the morning.
             That one was always thinking about the graveyard.
             "Maybe it's true people live after death;
             "Maybe when one dies,
                "one goes somewhere," he thought THIS WAY.
10   "Sure wish someone could tell me
                "if THESE BURIED ONES continue to exist."
             He would take some prayer meal
                then go to the mesa's edge
                and pray to THE SUN
15   saying
                   "Maybe you know
                   "if THE DEAD live.
                   "So if you know,
20   "tell me THIS."
                   That *one* went home,
                      but always *went there*
                      to pray that way.
          He went four times to pray
25   and sit at the place.
       Someone climbed up.
       The climber said to him,
       "Why do you want me?"
       "Yes," said *the sitter.*
30   "I always think ABOUT THESE BURIED ONES.
       "Is it possible that one really lives again?"

36

This one said,
"Yes.
"They live.
35 "It will be an ordeal,
"for you to see them."
That boy assented.
"Yes," he said.
"Very well," said the Sun.
40 "I will grant you THIS."
He handed him something.
"As soon as you go to sleep this evening,
"eat A LITTLE OF THIS."
"Tell *your parents* about it."
45 Thus he told the youth.
"I'll be getting along, "said the Sun.
That boy went home,
to his own house.
He got to the place,
50 and his mother was cooking.
After *those ones* had eaten,
he spoke to his father,
"My father?"
"Yes,
55 "what is it?"
"Yes," said *that boy*.
"When one dies,
"does one still exist?
"I wish to know this."
60 His mother said,
"Don't *do that*,
"but it is up to you," she said.
"Yes," said *that boy*.
"I will sleep deeply tonight,
65 "and I won't wake early," he said.
"The sun will come up
"and get overhead,
"but don't do anything to me;
"eventually I will return

70   "and waken."
           So his father said,
           "So be it."
           Night fell.
           He took a little of the medicine
75   and *doing that*
      that one fell asleep.
And *that one* really died:
      he drifted into the realm of the dead.
      That one came to Aponivi.
80   There was a great road.
He climbed the north face.
There someone sat.
That one had died some time ago.
"I know who that is," said the youth.
85   *That one* spoke,
      the one sitting at the place,
      "Are you from the place?"
      "Yes," said *that youth.*
      "Okay,
90   "let me get on your back," said
      that seated one.
        "Take me just four steps
         "and then set me *down.*"
     "No,
95   "I'm in a hurry," said *that youth.*
And *he* went on
      and *the one sitting*
        cried.
         When he had gone a little further,
100   again he came upon one sitting down.
      He said the same thing.
       Again *the youth* did not assent.
       He ascended to Bow Place.
There was also someone from life
105   carrying something.
It was a woman carrying a pebble on her back
with a bowstring as a tumpline

firmly embedded HERE in her scalp.
The woman said,
110 " take THIS for me."
"No," said the youth,
"I'm in a hurry."
That one went on,
and again there was
115 someone in the by-way.
That one was carrying a grinding stone
with a woman's hairstring as a tumpline.
On *one side of his feet* prickly pears were tied,
with cholla on the other
120 so he was not able to go very fast.
If he tried to go faster,
that one would really get pierced.
That one said,
"Take THIS from me."
125 "No," said the youth.
"I'm in a hurry."
That one went further
from the place *that one* ran real fast.
and came to a place
130 where there was a ringing.
It was an Agave Society member
who said,
"You've come?"
"Yes," said *that youth.*
135 And the Agave said,
"Did you see them?
"THIS IS THE WAY you wanted.
"So I will tell you about them.
"The first one you came to
140 "*that one* was very evil.
"When it was going to rain in the summer,
"*that one* prayed against it.
"He used something noxious to do something TO THE CLOUDS
"to make *them all* scatter.
145 "And the other one you came to

"that one killed someone.
"That one would shoot something bad in people
    · "so they would die.
"Those ones never get HERE.
150   *"Those ones* take four steps
"and sit *there.*
"THESE ONES are headed for Bow Place
"carrying things on their backs.
"Those ones take four steps
155   "and then sit *there.*
"Then *those ones* sit it out eight times,
"and then progress.
    "So they'll take a long time to reach HERE!
"Okay,
160   "get along!
"Go ALONG THIS WAY
"and as you get near
"you'll hear ringing somewhere."
So *he* went
165   towards the ringing
and again came upon someone
who said the same thing,
"You've come?"
"Yes," said *the youth.*
170   "Well,
"let's be off," said *the Agave Society member.*
He grasped the youth
and carried him along.
They came to where there was sobbing.
175   There was a fire roaring
at the place where *they* came.
It was a gaping hole
like a roasting pit
burning fiercely.
180   "Remember the ones you first came to?
"They come HITHER then
"I kill them HERE.
"The ones who were wicked at Oraibi,

          "I kill 'em HERE.

185   "One of them goes in

          "and *that one* catches on fire

          "turns to smoke

          "and goes back in.

             "Sometimes THIS PLACE is filled with smoke.

190   "*Such* is *their lot*:

       "*They* don't eat,

       "*They're* never happy.

       "They cared only for themselves.

       "Okay,

195   "let's be ON OUR WAY."

       They came to an opening somewhere;

         there wasn't a light anywhere.

       "I cast the remains HERE.

        "*They* stay at the place forever.

        "*They* never get out.

200   "Okay,

        "let's

        "go back.

       "THIS is what you wanted to see,"

       He took his hand.

205   They went back to *the other Agave member*.

       He said,

         "The two of you have come?"

         "Yes," said *the boy.*

        The road led TWO WAYS.

210   "Follow along here," said the Agave.

       He came to a village,

        a village of the dead.

        They existed only as white matter.

   Along the edge of the village walked another Agave.

215   He said,

       "You have come?

       "Okay,

        "come HITHER!"

       He took hold of him,

220   and they took him into the village.

    They arrived.
An Agave chief stood at the place
  at his house.
"You two have come?" he said.
225   "Yes," *they* replied together.
He said,
  "Well, come in!"
He grasped the youth in turn,
  that other Agave.
230   He went in.
    There were people sitting at the place.
He knew a person
who had been chief at Oraibi at one time.
  The Agave said
235   to the boy,
    "THIS is how THIS is;
    "THIS is what you wanted to know."
There, in a large flower,
  a deceased chief sat.
240 And three flowers
behind him also contained chiefs.
    "THIS IS HOW IT IS," said the Agave.
    "THESE were never not good at Oraibi;
    "they were always good.
245   "So they EXIST THIS WAY.
    "Okay,
    "now IT'S TIME for us to go."
  So they left.
There all kinds of grasses and plant
250   and all kinds of flowers.
    "IN THIS WAY they live," said the Agave.
    "THIS is what you wanted.
    "You will awaken here.
    "Okay,
255   "now you must go back!
    "You tell them how it is.
    "If one is not evil at Oraibi,
    "They come HERE.

       "THESE EVIL ONES don't COME HERE.
260   "You wake up!
       "Behold,
         "*there is a road* planned for them.
       "When you get back,
         "you tell them
265   "all about OUR LIVING HERE THIS WAY.
       "One thinks of the group's
         "abiding.
       "THIS is what you wanted.
       "You entered our village,
270 "you know all about it.
       "If you ever feel like coming back
       "eat from your medicine.
         "But now THESE ONES: your mother,
         "your father,
275   "tell them ABOUT THIS.
  "They are never *that* way.
       "The one who doubts my word will not abide HERE with the others.
       "Okay,
       "be off!
280   "Run!
       "Your mother
         "and father,
         "*those ones* are waiting for you!"
         And so *from there he* really ran.
285   He came to the Agave chief,
  at the fork in the road.
    He said,
       "You've come?"
       "Yes," said the youth.
290   "So be it.
       "You really run for it!"
       "Your mother,
         "your father,
         "*they* are waiting."
295   *That one* ran directly from the place.
         He came to Bow Place

where recall *those ones* were atoning,
those damn thieves,
those ones were trying to get to the Underworld
300   but were atoning *there.*
They were afraid that
  by and by their salve would run out and
    and they would arrive in the Underworld at no sure time.
  After *those two* got to the place,
305   *that seated Agave* said,
    "From here, you're on your own."
  "Yes," said the youth.
He really ran.
He came to the woman
310 who said to him,
  "How fortunate you are to return."
  "Yes," said the youth.
Then again he was running
He came to the north face of Aponivi to the killer
315   "Lucky you to come back," said the atoner.
  "Yes,"
was all *that youth* said,
  and off he ran.
  He came to the foothills of Aponivi
320   to *the one who wanted no rain.*
That one said *the same* as the other
"Yes," said *that youth*
  running on
    arriving at his own house
325   at Oraibi,
    entering his body,
      just as the sun was coming up
and awoke.
  He sat up
330 and just sat *there*
  thinking.
The sun was climbing in the sky
  and his mother had been cooking
    and looked in on him.

335   "Are you awake?" asked *his mother.*
        "Yes."
        "Okay,
           "we're going to eat,
        "so come OVER HERE."
340   *The boy* replied affirmatively.
        They were eating
        and after *they* had finished,
           his father asked *that boy,*
             "So what did you find out?"
345   "Yes," said the youth.
        "They really do exist.
        "I saw everything in the world of the dead.
        "A chief at the place told me THIS,
           "WHAT I am telling you.
350   "The Agave chief burns THE EVILS ONES at the place.
           "THEIR LIKES never see the light of day.
              "THE ONES who were chiefs HERE
                 "live well at the place,
           "and are *chiefs* at the place.
355   "THIS IS WHAT I saw of their life at the place.
        "So THIS IS WHY if the two of you ever fail to wake me,
           "you'll have no reason to worry.
        "They really do exist after death."
        THIS he told them.
360   So *they* went on living.
        He brooded about going back,
        He spoke to his father,
           "Our father,
              "our mother!"
365   "Yes," *they* said.
        "I'm going to go back."
        "Okay," said *the father.*
           That night *he* took a little of his medicine
              and *he* fell asleep
370   and *he* really died.
              The parents were eating,
                 and when they had eaten,

they looked in on the boy.
He was dead,
375   so *they* had to wrap *him* up.
So *they* went to place *him* below at Kuyvö.
They buried him.
They all continued to live on.
Yet *they both,*
380   the father and mother
missed
the boy.
The father went to the fields,
and *he* got to his field,
385   and was hoeing.
Something was running ALONG THERE,
it was some kind of bird,
a sandpiper.
And *the sandpiper* spoke to him,
390   "Poor you," it said.
"My poor father misses me."
The father spoke,
"Yes,
"I do miss you."
395   "Don't *do that*," it said.
"Remember what I told you.
"In four days' time I'll be back;
"so be sure to come together," it said,
and ran away.
400   On the fourth day
the father said to the mother,
"We should go together to the field."
His wife fixed a lunch.
They went there.
405   *They* arrived,
and were hoeing
when *the husband* said to *his wife,*
"Maybe someone will stop by."
"Who?" she asked.
410   They were still talking LIKE THIS

when it arrived.
A call came from nearby.
It ran up to them.
It came towards them,
415   and when it got there,
that one said "pity;"
"You miss me."
The father said,
"Yes!"
420   "Well, *don't do that.*
"I'm fine."
And the mother said,
"Yes,
"I miss you."
425   "But,
"don't be like that," it said.
"I will not get to look in on you again."
Saying only that,
it ran away from there again.
430   *They* went home in the evening.
Whenever the father went to the field,
he would always stop there.
They just went on living.

❚

THIS IS ALL.

The setting function in "Maskimiqw" is dealt with very briefly in lines 1 and 2. In line 3, the stage is set for the protagonist's desire: he wonders about the fate of the dead. A cluster of proximals (lines 7, 9, 11, 14, 17, 20) mark his pondering and consequent prayers to the Sun. The Sun arrives as the plan function begins in line 30 with a string of proximal references, but the Sun's actual consent to help the youth is given in line 40 and marked with a proximal there and again in line 43. The journey function begins around line 75. Although there is no proximal marking at that point, it does occur each time he meets someone in the Underworld: in line 110, he meets a wicked woman; in line 124, a sorcerer who has taken the lives of others; in line 136 an Agave Society member (a society in charge of the afterlife). In lines 143, 152, 158, and 161, the wicked are lambasted. The exception is the very first malfeasant the youth meets (line 100). In a cluster of proximals (lines 181, 182, 184, 189), the youth is shown the fire pit where the wicked will end up.

In another cluster of proximals (lines 236, 237, 242, 245, 251, 252), the youth briefly visits the Land of the Blessed, specifically witnessing the happy condition of former chiefs who served their people well. The return journey begins with another cluster of proximal markers (lines 258, 259, 265, 268, 273, 277); here is the beginning of the end, the realization of a visit to the afterlife. This cluster revolves around several messages:

> this is what you wanted to know;
> this is where they all come;
> tell your parents and others about this;
> don't be selfish.

The last cluster of proximals (lines 348, 349, 350, 351, 352, 355, 356) occurs where the boy repeats the messages to his parents. It is remarkable in that the only natural way to translate most of these proximals at the end of a story into English is with 'they,' 'what,' and 'where' (instead of 'these,' 'this way,' and 'here,' as in the Hopi text); proximals have some highlighting pragmatic force in English (as they do in Hopi), but lack a summarizing effect.

The last two proximals (lines 386, 410) mark the return of the boy as a plover to reassure each of his parents in turn.

In this example, several important extensions of proximal marking are illustrated. Proximals are not necessarily found at the exact beginning of a section, but occur within a maximum of ten lines from the beginning. Personal names and place-names may occur as first mentions, so they have the rhetorical force of proximals. Clusters of proximals serve to create a highlighting texture within the fabric of the story. Single proximal markers may be used to point up particular single incidents in the story (as in the persons met in the Underworld, and at the end when the plover meets each parent in turn).

SECOND MESA TEXTS

The narrative conventions of Third Mesa (Oraibi) stories (almost all of the published texts are in the Third Mesa dialect) also occur in narratives from other Hopi villages. Edward Kennard, for example, collected a Second

Mesa version of "The Journey to the Underworld" in 1934. His version was told by Frank Masakwaftiwa and translated by Ann Mae Setima (Kennard 1989), and of texts in Second Mesa (Mishongnovi) dialect collected by Kennard.

To illustrate that the approach developed here applies equally to texts from other dialect traditions, the first section of the story is quoted here; see also "Lolenso," below. This section, which is representative of the story, follows the same narrative conventions as Third Mesa narratives. I have retranscribed Kennard's typescript text; the translation is my own.

> Yaw Orayve yeesiwa.
> Niq yaw ev haakim naanatim ki'yungwa,
>   suukya tiyo niq suukya maana.
> Tiyo yaw Honanyestiwa
> 5 niq pu' maana Honanyesnöma,
>   YAN yaw puma maatsiwa.
> Yaw *puma* Kwaangyam.
> Niq yaw *pam tiyo* pay yaw pas hiita qa'emingwu
>   yaw sutsev Paamuylalwa.
> 10 Niq yaw *pam* pay qa haq aqw'a . . .
> Yaw as *pam* tuwat hin hak mooke'
>   hintingwu.
> Put yaw as pa tuwat pas hin navotiniqa'e
>   naawakna.
> 15 Niq pangqa'e Orayvi hovqövaqa'e
>   yaw tutu'ami pangsoq yaw pam oovi kuyvatongwu,
>   pu' Taawat enang piw aw'i,
>   *pam* yaw as sen piw hin a'awnaniqö.
> Yaw oovi su'aw naalösni'maqw
> 20 ev pu' yaw aw Taawa nakwsu.
> Pas yaw hak su'hìmu taaqa lomayuwsita,
>   yaw'i.
> "Is oki um'u," kita aw'i.
> "Owi," pu' yaw pam aw kita.
> 25 "Hintiqw um tuwat pas hin *put* tuwat navotniqa'e
>   "naawakna?"
> "Owi," pu' yaw pan tuwat aw kita.
> "Owi,

"pay as YEV antsa IMA TOOTIM maamantuy amum haalayyaqw
30   "pay nu' tuwat qa hin aqw haqami kuyvaniqa'e
"unàngwtingwuy," pam aw kita.

𝟙

They were living at Oraibi.
Some people lived at the place with children,
    a boy and a girl.
The boy was Honanyestiwa,
5   and the girl Honanyesnöma;
    THIS WAY they were called.
Those ones were Agave Clan.
And *the boy* went nowhere,
    even though they had social dances in January.
10   *He* never went . . .
If *he* should die,
    what would it be like?
That is what
    (he) wanted to know.
15   On the east slope of Oraibi toward the graves
    (he) went to look (at them),
        and to the Sun
        he prayed.
Right on the fourth day
20   the Sun came
As a handsome man,
    handsomely dressed.
"Poor you," he said.
"Yes," the boy said.
25   "Why do you want to know *that?*"
    said the Sun
"Yes," said the boy.
"Yes," he said,
"THESE BOYS are happy HERE with girls,
30   but I never feel like
        going to the kiva with them."

The first section of this myth concentrates on the boy. He, his sister, and his preoccupation with death are the discourse topics in the first section. In line 6, "THIS WAY" establishes the newness of the sibling pair as a topic, and in line 7 they become "those ones." In four mentions (lines 8, 10, 11, and 19), the boy is coded with distal deictics. In line 25, his preoccupation with death is coded as "*that.*" The section reports his situation and the plan he makes that will take him on a journey away from home base. In line 29, the new section begins with "THESE BOYS . . . HERE"; here the journey to the Underworld begins.

Although Kennard's Second Mesa version takes a different focus, the Hopi narrative schema is followed and sections are delineated with proximal deixis. A comparison of the two versions of the myth suggests that individual narrators are free to define focus and sectionality in their own performances, but that the narrative schema and sectioning convention must be followed. In Voth's version, sections corresponded closely to the narrative functions; in Kennard's comparatively longer version, with more "time" to tell the story, the motivation of the boy is dwelt upon in the first part of the narrative.

THE ADAPTATION OF BIBLICAL NARRATIVES

Further corroboration of the model of Hopi narrative discourse proposed here is provided by examining narratives that have been translated from English to Hopi by native speakers with the assistance of missionaries. The only sustained effort in this regard is the New Testament (New Testament 1983). The parables in the Hopi translation conform to another Hopi pattern: the use of indirection to enjoin or admonish; indirection is addressed at length in chapter 4.

The deictic marking of sections is used in the New Testament translation when a long narrative sequence occurs. Moreover, the Hopi sections do not always correspond to the traditional chapter divisions. When an especially important long narrative is translated, the use of marked spatial deixis is used in the Hopi translation as a sectioning device. A good example is the Passion related in John. Here there are three sections. The first two are framed with proximals at the beginning and end. Discourse topics within each section are marked by distal deictics. I will discuss the rhetorical structure of the Hopi translation with reference to the accompanying King James Version. Additional reference will be made to the Greek text (Marshall 1975), although the Greek text could not have been used exclusively in the Hopi translation.

The first section deals with the retreat of Jesus and some disciples to the Mount of Olives.

1. YAN Jesus lavàytit, put aw
   nánatuwnayaqamuy tsamkyangw pàapiy
   nakwsuqw, puma haqe' sikya Cedron
   YAN matsìwqat yupqöymi pítùuqe
   put aw nánatuwnayaqamuy pangso paki . . .
9. Ura pam hingqàwq put àntiniqw oovi'o
   ura pam pangqawu: IMUY hakimuy um inumi
   no'aqw nu qa hììtaqat kwahi, IT'A
   (New Testament 1983:382)

𝕚

1. When Jesus had spoken these words, he
   went forth with his disciples over the
   brook Cedron, where there was a garden, into the
   which he entered, and his disciples . . .
9. that the saying might be fulfilled,
   which he spake, Of them which thou gavest me,
   I have none.

There are two proximals at the beginning of this passage.

(a) YAN Jesus lavàytit (for "when Jesus had spoken")
(b) Cedron YAN maatsìwqa (for "the brook Cedron")

Discounting (b), because proximal marking is ordinarily required with *maatsiwa*, 'be called,' this leaves (a) to establish the beginning of a section; note that (a) is not required by the English text (though it is present in the Greek text: "having spoken these things").

The closing of the first section, quoted above in verse 9, is signaled by a proximal that has no equivalent in English or in the Greek text (*imuy*, 'these ones,' objective case), by a different-subject marker (-*qw*), and by a second proximal that has no equivalent in the English text (*it'a*, 'this one') in a marked phonological shape (which has a summarizing effect; *it*, 'this' normally would not occur finally, but when it does, it has the marked form *it'a*). This marked proximal is not required in the Greek

52

text or the English version. This use of *it'a*, called here **pausalization**, highlights the rhetorical force of 'this' even more.

The next section begins with a proximal marking a new mention.

10. Pàasat pu' Simon Peter sipwuvàapi'ytaqe
putvaqw naqvuyat ayó tuku. Noqw I' hak
tuuwiki Malchus YAN maatsiwa . . . [3 verses]

14. I' Caiphas hapi ura Jew sinmuy
amumi pangqawu: Pay ura hak suukya sinmuy
amungem mokq pam ngas'ewniqata.
(New Testament 1983:384)

🔲

10. Then Simon Peter, having a sword drew it,
and cut off his [another person's] right ear.
The servant's name was Malchus . . . [3 verses]

14. It was Caiphas who had given counsel to
the Jews, that it was expedient that one
man should die for the people.

The new mention is the servant Malchus, marked with the proximal *i'*, 'this one'; the proximal is not required by either the Greek or English text. Malchus is mentioned later in the section (in verse 26), as a relative of his approaches Simon Peter to question him about his connection with Jesus; the second mention of Malchus (*pam hapi Malchus*, 'that one indeed called Malchus [the very one]') is coded with the distal *pam*.

The mention of the High Priest, Caiphas, in verse 14 is marked with a proximal that is not required in either the Greek text or the English translation. This is the first appearance of Caiphas in this narrative.

The third section begins with Jesus being coded only by a proximal (*it*) which is used alone (the Greek and English both have 'this man' instead of simply 'this' in Hopi). In the subsequent mention of Jesus in verse 30, the full noun phrase *it taaqat*, 'this man' is used where the source texts have simply 'he.'

29. Pàasat pu' Rome angqw mongwi Pilate
YAN maatsìwqa yámakqe amumi pangqawu:
Ya uma hìita IT neeveltoynaya?"

30. Noqw puma lavàytotiqe aw pangqawu:
    "Pay pi as I' taaqa qa nukpananiqw so'on
    itam uumi put wikvayani." (N.T., p. 386)

◪

29. Pilate went out unto them, and said,
    "What accusation do you have against
    this man?"
30. They answered and they said to him,
    "If he were not a malefactor, we would
    not have delivered him up unto thee."

The new mention of Jesus at the beginning of the section (the *it* of the last line of verse 29) is mandated by both the English and Greek texts. Yet one clause later, Jesus is coded with another proximal (*i' taaqa*, 'this man') for the English 'he.' The next mention of Jesus is three clauses away, and is marked with distal deixis. Native sectioning persists, supported by the source text(s) in this instance.

The chapter of the English text (John, chapter 18) ends with a new mention.

> . . . Noq I' Barabbas pi hìita tuunàwkilawu.
> (New Testament 1983:387)

◪

> . . . Now Barabbas was a robber.

The proximal here (*i'*) is not in the English or Greek text. Barabbas is the person who was freed in place of Jesus, and is thus an important mention. Hence, the Hopi translator has logically begun a new section despite the lack of fit with the traditional chapter division. The saliency of spatial deictic marking of sections is carried over from Hopi rhetoric, even though the narrative itself does not conform to the semantic portion of the Hopi narrative schema, which always casts the plot as a journey.

Hopi translators, carefully working their way through the English text, made use of native rhetoric. Such a "persistence" imparts to the translation a feeling of validity and authority. Formal genres in other preliterate cultures create and sustain solidarity and group identity (Urban 1986). The use of native rhetoric in novel discourses serves to naturalize the novel genre(s) produced (Hanks 1987). It is significant that the mechanics of the Hopi narrative schema and the symbolic functions of those mechanics in this instance validate novel Hopi discursive practice.

2

HOPI NARRATIVE VERSIFICATION

IN HOPI TRADITIONAL NARRATIVES, as we have seen, spatial deictics are typically used in a marked opposition to establish sectional boundaries. Hopi traditional narratives can be sectioned into **lines** (usually a clause) and groups of lines defined by subordination of clauses with initial particles and verb suffixes. The resulting lines tend to form sets of four (quatrains) that are rhetorically significant. Scansion conventions (see table 2.1, below) are traditional, as are the other defining characteristics of Hopi narration; versification is not entirely a function of individual stylistic preference, in contrast to the texts analyzed by Hymes (1981).

Using texts of narratives that represent true performances (see Bauman 1986) of traditional Native American stories, Dell Hymes (1981) uncovers a poetic structure consisting of parallel units (couplets, triplets, etc.) organized in a rhetorically consistent hierarchy. Hymes used a "particle" approach; grammatical particles, conjunctions, and other syntactic devices are used as cues to discourse structure. Tedlock (1983) employs a prosodic solution to the same problem by relying on intonation cues and pausing. The two approaches tend to coincide (Bright 1979, Kroskrity 1985), because of the cognitive demands of discourse processing; where the two systems of sectioning, for example, do not coincide, the differences often carry rhetorical significance (Woodbury 1987).

Dell Hymes has shown that different narrators in the same speech community, using the same linguistic code and performing in the same formal genre, produce different ethnopoetic structures. The analyst, following the results of Hymes's research, is thus cautioned not to seek a parsing algorithm:

> what cannot be stressed too much, is that Hymes' method is not to be thought of as a cookie cutter that you impress on a narrative . . . [one cannot] just look for initial particles [or other grammatical features] . . . what is involved is a patient working back and forth between content and form (V. Hymes 1987:68–69).

In Hopi culture, with its strong communal orientation, however, versification, like other aspects of narrative style, is partly predictable.

In Dell Hymes's approach to ethnopoetic research, single lines (usually a clause in length) are gathered into couplets, triplets, etc., to create a rhetorical structure "of cultural (and personal) style" (1987:19). For example, in Chinookan texts, Hymes has found a rhetorical movement he calls "onset-ongoing-outcome." Verses or groups of verses realize these three narrative functions, which comprise a category of Chinookan culture. The mechanics of marking the units, however, vary. The Wishram Chinook stories of Louis Simpson are overtly marked in accordance with the same onset-ongoing-outcome model as the Clackamas Chinook texts of Victoria Howard, but the latter narratives only sometimes have overt markers of versification (D. Hymes 1987:20). The Chinookan rhetorical pattern, much like the Hopi narrative schema, is a salient item in the culture, so much so that it persists into ordinary conversation in English: in a restaurant conversation about rising food prices, Hiram Smith (Wasco Chinook) remarked, "What can you do? You buy, you pay, you get out" (D. Hymes 1987:20). It is important to note that while the Chinookan narrative schema is a constant, the mechanics for realizing it may vary.

Hymes's system of versification distinguishes two loci (individual and collective or cultural) and two kinds of patterning (rhetorical and mechanical). Variation, which is the source of much of the aesthetics of an art form, occurs on the individual level. The opposite is true in Hopi narrative practice (table 2.2).

TABLE 2.1. RHETORICAL PATTERNING IN
CHINOOKAN AND HOPI NARRATIVE

	Chinookan	Hopi
mechanics	individual	collective
rhetoric	collective	individual

Concepts of Hopi narrative mechanics (including versification) are collectively held; acceptable variation lies in fitting the rhetorical pattern
(a story = a journey) into the common structural units.

In his single analysis of a Hopi text, Dell Hymes noted that the numeral
four is significant in Hopi narratives (D. Hymes 1992). His analysis, which
began by identifying verses indicated by the quotative *yaw* and the particle *pu'* ('now/finally/then'), then grouping verses into larger units, distinguishes four "acts" in Helen Sekaquaptewa's "Coyote and the Birds."
Each "act" has four "scenes." His analysis is completely compatible with
the one presented here, which proceeds from small- to large-scale features, with lines predictably gathering into quatrains.

I will analyze one Hopi traditional narrative using the scansion convention
presented in table 2.2. This is one possible convention; the other possibilities are using initial particles only, or else using the verb suffixes as the
only criteria for scansion based on subordination. This is called a "possible" scansion convention for four reasons: (1) different conventions yield
different quatrains with the purely "particle" approach of Hymes and Tedlock
(see chapter four); (2) until the entire extant body of texts has been analyzed with respect to versification, a definitive approach cannot be given;
(3) I have used a single one here for the sake of consistency; (4) the one
used here is based both on particles (*pu'* and conjunctions beginning with
ni- except for *niqw* and *noqw*, and subordinating verb suffixes).

The text was spontaneously elicited, then translated and edited as a
flat text. The results of this versification match the deictically defined
sections in function.

TABLE 2.2. A POSSIBLE HOPI SCANSION CONVENTION

0. The basic unit is the line, usually one clause in length.
1. Initial *pu'* and initial conjunctions in *ni(i)-* are subordinating (but not

niq(w) or *noqw*), as are the conjunctive verb suffixes (*-qe, -e', -kyangw, -t, -qw*), which subordinate the following line.

2. Subordinate clauses are indented; each succeeding subordinated clause is correspondingly indented.

3. Quotations and quotation tags ("s/he said") following a quotation are subordinated as a single line. Relative clauses are part of the clause (line) in which they occur, unless they are pausalized.

4. Pausalized clauses/lines are subordinate, as are appositives that are pausalized or of two or more words in length. Interjections at the beginning of a sentence may form a separate line, with the following line being subordinate to the line with the interjection.

Both initial particles and conjunctive predicate suffixes are subordinating (Shaul 1987b). Subordination is recursive; succeeding subordinate lines are subordinate to immediately preceding lines. Four is the ritual number of Hopi culture, and the scansion convention tends to produce units of four.

"COYOTE AND WREN"

The beginning of the first example text (Seumptewa, Voegelin, and Voegelin 1980) is relatively short. The story was told, and the English translation of each was also elicited on the spot. It has almost no spatial deictic marking; consequently, it serves as a useful way of testing the rhetoric associated with the deictic model of Hopi traditional narratives. The lack of spatial deictics appears to be a feature of unplanned or unrehearsed Hopi narratives. In other sentences, particles are used as discourse continuers (similar in function but not context to *well, um,* and *uh* in informal conversations in English); examples include *yaw* repeated in line 35 and *pu'* repeated in line 39. Note that the story lacks an ending formula.

COYOTE AND WREN
Haliksay.

𝟭

Yaw Ismo'walpe yeesiwa.
Noqw yaw pep Iisaw ki'yta
  pu' yaw piw Orayve yeesiwa.

59

5   Noqw yaw Orayve atkya kiitavangw yaw piw Tutsvo ki'yta.
       Yaw korongaqw pam ki'yta.
       Noqw yaw Iisaw naalöqmuy tiimu'yta
          nìiqe yaw pam pangqw paami tiimuy amungem kuytongwu
          niikyangw yaw put Tutvot kiyat aqle' ngwuniqw
10   sutsep pam Tutsvo kiy ìipaq tawkyangw
          wunimangwunikyangw
          taya'iwtangwu.
       Noqw yaw Iisaw tiimuy amungem kuyte'
          pu' paave paamoytat
15   pu' pangqw paamoykyangw
          nimangwu.
       Niqw yaw Tutsvot kiyat ìipo pituq
          piw pay yaw Tutsvo hin'ur wunimakyangw
          taya'iwta.
20   Pay yaw Iisaw aw tunatyawte'
          pay yaw tayate'
          pay sòosok paamoyiy wehekna
          pu' yaw Tutsvot aw itsivu'iwta
          pu' yaw pam piw nawus ahoy paamini.
25   Noqw yaw hìisakis pam paamoykyangw
          pam pangso pituq
          yaw soq Tutsvo taya'iwkyangw
          wunimakyangw
          tsotso'tinumq
30   piw pay yaw Iisaw aw tayate'
             piw pay kuuyiy sòosok paamoywutangwu.
       Nuwu yaw timu'at so'on haqam qa paanaqso'iwtaq
          pu' yaw timu'at so'on haqam qa paanaqso'iwtaqw
          pu' yaw Iisaw Tutsvot aw itsivoti.
35   Yaw paapu qa wunimaqat yaw aw kita,
          pu' yaw Tutsvo naawini
       yaw pam yaw naayukuqe
          tukpuy ang yaw put qalavit tangata
             nìiqe pu' yaw pam pàasat pu' haqam tsokingwu
40   nìiqe pangsoq put tsoka.
       Noqw yaw Iisaw piw angniqw

pu' piw pay ayw put tayatoynaqw
noqw yaw aw pangqawu
"Yaw um nuy piw tayatoynaqw
45   "pu' nu pay so'on ung qa sowani," yaw aw kita.
Noqw pu' yaw pay antsa qavongvaqw piw pam kuytoqw
piw pay yaw Tutsvo epnikyangw
yaw ang oongaqw tsokiwta.
·   Naato yaw as pay qa hìntiqw
50   pay yaw pam tayatiqe'
pay itsivotiqe
yaw hin'ur Iisaw itsivo'iwtaqe
pu' yaw pay Tutsvot yòotoqe
put ngaroròyku.
55   Noqw yaw pay pam pep aqlap haqam owat aakwayngya haqam na'uyi'yta.
Yaw pam taya'iwta.
Pas hapi yaw Iisaw put ngaroroveveta.
Pay pi yaw pam owat tukpuy ang mokyàataqw
pu' nìiqe niqw pavan yaw Iisaw ungwtsangwta.
60   Noqw pàasat pu' yaw pay pam pangkyang paami piw yaw pam kuyniqe
paamoytaniqe
motòltiqw
yaw angqw aw himu nùutsel'eway tayta.
Yaw pam kur qa hìita kuuyit.
65   Pay pangqw piw sutsvo paami
nìiqe pu' yaw pam piw pangso paamiqw
piw pangqw kuyniqw
tayata;
pu' yaw pam piw pangqw pàasat piw naat sutsvo paami
70   pu' yaw pam àasakis paami pituqw
pam himu nùutsel'eway angqw kya pi kuytangwu,
himu yaw ungwtsangwtakyango.
Noqw pu' yaw pam hin'ur paamiq itsivo'iwta.
"Ya um hìntiqw nuy qa hikwna?
75   "Ya um paahut kyàakyawnaqe oovi'o," yaw kita.
Yaw nawus pam qa ahoy timuy aw kuuyi'yma.
Naat kya pam oovi angqe paahepnuma.
Sen pi haqam paanaqmoki.

COYOTE AND WREN
Listen.

𝟚

They were living at Coyote Gap.
  Coyote was living there
    and they were living at Oraibi,
5   and below Oraibi south of the village Wren was living.
It was a rock cranny in which she lived.
Coyote had four pups,
  so she'd go from there to get water for them.
  Coyote had to go by Wren's house.
10   Wren was always there singing outside her house
      dancing around
        laughing.
So when Coyote went to get water for her pups,
  after getting water in her mouth at the spring,
15   as she came from there mouthing the water
      on her way home,
she'd come to outside of Wren's house
  and Wren would be dancing it up,
    laughing.
20 Well, if Coyote took notice of her
    and if she laughed,
      she'd spill her mouthed water
        and get mad at Wren
        and have to go back to the spring.
25 As she repeatedly went mouthing water,
    arriving there,
      inevitably Wren would be laughing
        dancing,
          jumping all over.
30   If Coyote laughed,
        she'd lose all her mouthed water.
The pups must have been getting thirsty all the while
  and with her pups dying of thirst and all,
    Coyote got mad at Wren.
35 Told her she'd better not dance.

So Wren planned
to make an image of herself
and put gravel in a bag of hers
and so then where she usually sat,
40   there she set it up.
So Coyote passed by again
and again she just had to laugh and
so she said,
"Better not make me laugh,
45   "or else I'll sure gobble you all up."
So the very next day she was coming to get water and
again Wren was there
perched up above.
Before she could do anything
50   Coyote laughed
and got mad
and in anger
grabbed that Wren
and crunched 'er up.
55   Hidden behind a rock way to the side,
Wren was laughing.
Coyote was sure crunching away, and
since the bag had rocks in it,
it's no surprise Coyote had a bloody mouth.
60   Then she went again to the spring to get water
and when she got some water in her mouth,
having stooped down to drink,
there was this frightful thing looking at her.
She didn't get any water
65   and went to another spring
and when she got there
to get a drink of water
there it was looking at her.
So she went off to another spring
70   and when she got to the spring
the thing was there getting a drink,
that thing with the bloody mouth.
She got real mad at the spring.

"Why don't you let me get myself a drink?
75   "You hogging the spring—is that it?"
She must not have gotten back to her pups with water,
and maybe she's still out there looking for water.
Or maybe she just died somewhere of thirst.

Before discussing the quatrains, it should be noted that some adjacent lines that are semantically coordinate or synonymous are treated as couplets for purposes of scansion.

10/11	"sing**ing** and danc**ing**"
20/21	"**if** Coyote noticed and **if** she laughed"
28/29	"**dancing** and **jumping**"
51/52	"got **mad** and **in anger**"

A couplet is formed when both predicates have the same conjunctive ending (10/11, 20/21, 51/52) or the same predicate root (28/29). These couplets all function as single lines in quatrains. Paired synonymous constructions, then, are treated as a single line. Dell Hymes (1994 and 1995:128) found instances in a Wishram Chinook and a Takelma text where treating couplets as single units for patterning in stanzas was the key to consistent organization at certain points.

A list of the quatrains in this narrative is provided with paraphrases in table 2.3. Given the initial setting of Coyote passing Wren's house to and from the spring to get water for her pups, the reader can easily follow the story from the quatrains. About two-thirds of all the lines in the story form quatrains.

TABLE 2.3. QUATRAINS IN "COYOTE AND WREN"

lines	summary
8–12	Coyote gets water; Wren dances.
13–16	Coyote carries water in mouth.
20–24	Coyote sees Wren, spills water.
25–29	Coyote comes with water; Wren dances.
37–40	Wren puts rocks in bag decoy.
42–45	Coyote warns Wren.
50–54	Coyote gets mad, crunches Wren.

55–58	Wren laughs at Coyote.
60–63	Coyote stoops to drink, sees an ugly thing.
65–68	Coyote goes to another spring.
69–72	The thing is still there.

The coyote story represents spontaneous storytelling; the performance was not planned beforehand. Nonetheless, the subordination creates a complex textual architecture for the storyline that has striking semantic and rhetorical motivation.

For example the first four quatrains all repeat the same scene from a different perspective. In the first quatrain (8–12), Coyote passes by to get water and notices Wren dancing and singing about; this initially reports the scene and situation for the entire story. The second quatrain (13–16) focuses on Wren, but then has Coyote enter with water in her mouth. In the third quatrain (20–24), as Coyote watches, Wren is laughing at Coyote's mouthed water. In the next quatrain (25–29), the viewpoint of both actors is again reported by way of summing up the action to come.

"LOLENSO"

In order to illustrate the function of versification with a longer text, I have selected a story that relates how the Snake Dance came to Oraibi; it differs from the more usual tradition that a certain Tiyo rafted down the Colorado River to the Land of the Snakes, married there, and then brought the Snake Dance back with his family to Hopi. The present text is also a migration tradition. It combines historical tradition with mythical force and so is both legend and myth. The story lacks a beginning formula, which has been added.

LOLENSO (VOTH N.D.)
[Aliksay.]

𝟏

Pay hisat yaw Yungyawtsayve yeesiwa.
Niq yaw hak lomamana qa haki yaw naawakna.
Niq pu' yaw tootim naanawakna,
   pu' yaw tootim awya[qw]
5   niq qa haki naawakna.

Niq yaw hin'eway tiyo yaw panis so'ta,
    yaw'i.
Niq yaw pam tuwat lomamanat aw'i.
Niq pay yaw aw'i,
10   naawakna.
Pay yaw *put* nöömata.
Pay yaw tootim itsivutoti.
    Pu' yaw pay nawkiyani,
        hin'ewayo.
15   "Itam nawkiyani,
        "oovi itam makwisni:
        "wuuhaq qöyaqa nömayat ev pituni,
            "tavkyiqö."
    Pu' makwisqw
20   lomamanat kongya'at wuuhaq qöya.
    Pay nawis nöömay ev pitu
        pu' yaw payya[q]
            itsivutoti[qe]
                [pangqaqwu]
25   "Pu itam pas nawkiyani."
    "Ayo' taatö Höövatuyqami wukotsu'a YAASAYA,
        "pev *pam* ki'ta.
    "Put oovi aw wiktoni.
    "Aw wiktoq
30   "pay ev *put* niinani.
    "Niq itam nöömayatyani."
    Pay aw tuu'awma,
        pu' ev pitu.
        "Um hintsaknuma?"
35   "Pay nu' angqw tuu'awma."
        "Hita'a?"
        "Pi um ayo' Höövatuyqami wukotsu'at itamungem wiktoni."
        "Ha'owi?
            "Hintsaq oovi'o?"
40   "Um wikvàq
            "itam aw yorikyani[q]
                "hinpi pas soniwa.
            "Qa hak aw yorik[q]

66

      "hinpi pas soniwa."
45   "Ta'ay,
      "pay pi nu aw wiktoni."
   Pu' yaw aw wikto,
     pu' aw warikiwta.
   Aqw tuupok pitu.
50   "Is uti,
      "nuwupa
        "nu aw pitùni[q]
        "so'on pi nuy qa niinani," yaw wuuwanma.
   Okiwa naat wuuwanmaq
55   pay haqaq hak hingqawu,
      "Imöyhoya,
      "um haqami'i?"
   "Pi nu YUKYIQ oomiq wukotsu'at nu wikto."
   "Haaki.
60   "Um pewni."
   Pu' aw'i.
   "Okiwa,
     "imöyhoya.
   "*Pam* hakiy niinangwu.
65   "Niq oovi um IT yawmani,"
     pu' yaw ngahuyi maqa.
   "Um aqw pite'
     "um *put* moytani,
      "pu' umi itsivuyiwtani,
70   "pu' um IT AW pavoyani.
   "YANTINI,
     "me.
   "Niq pay qa itsivuyiwtani.
   "Pay um aw pitùni."

▮

75   "Um hintsaknuma?"
   "Pay nu ung aw wikto."
   "Ha'owi?
    "Hinoq'ö?"
   "Pi yaw pev Yungyatsayve tuupak kivayungqam umi yorikyaniq

67

80   "*puma pan* naanawakna
        "niiqa'e nuy ayatota.
        "Nu ung wiktoniqat inumi naanawakna.
        "Niq oovi nu ung wikto."
        "Antsa'a,
85   "pay nu umumni.
        "Haaki,
          "ason nuy yuwsito."
        Pu' kivay aqw paki,
          pu' yaw kwiniwiq nakwsu,
90   pu' yaw YAASUK kuysivut kwusu,
            pu' yaw put angqw kyaalat kuuyiwta.
        Put yaw angqw hiiko.
        Piw yaw sukya'a.
        Kuysivut piw yaw kwusu.
95   Piw yaw angqw hiiko.
        A'ne hiiko.
          "Hapi yantani.
          "Tum'uy,
            "haqam ung nuutayungwa.
100   "Um pay nuy iikwiwtani,
          "pi nu a'ne hikwqa'e
            "nu puutu."
        Angqw pu' *put* yaw *pam* iikwiwta.
        Kiimiq iikwiwta.
105   Pas yaw a'ne puutu.
        Panmakyang
          kiihut aw pitu.
        Pay wukotsu'at aw pangqawu,
          "Ta'ay,
110   "um töqmani."
          Pu' yaw töqti.
            "Pew uma nay tu'sawwisni," yaw kita.
            "Taq pay nuy angwumay,
              "oovi uma nuy tu'sawwisni."
115   Pu' yaw aqw tumpok kukuyvaq
                hak töqma.
        Pay yaw wukotsu'a a'ne yaw siyiyoyota.

Pas pay yaw aya.
   Pu' yaw pay àapiy watqa,
120   kivamiq yaw pay a'awnaya,
     YANGQW wukotsu'at Lolenso iikwiwta[qe]
     kur piw qa niina.
Pay yaw *puma* qa haalaytoti.
Pay yaw YAN okwayyungwa.
125   Taataqt kyaastaq wukotangawta,
     kivape.
Pumuy aw wikva.
Amumiq aw tsa'lawu,
   "Haw I'IVI,
130   "nu YEV umungem wikva.
"Uma IT hintsanyaniqa'e
   "naanawakna?"
Qa hak hingqawu.
Puma taataqt tsaatsawna[q]
135   pu' yaw *pam* wukotsu'at pay aqw kivamiq pu' tavi.
Niqw yaw a'ne ayayatoya[q]
   pu' yaw *puma sinom* ev nanavta.
    "YAPIHAQ YAN Lolenso wukotsu'at wikva.
    "Owi,
140   "tuma kuyvawwisni."
     Pu' yaw yuyutya.
Antsa YAASAVO yaw wunu.
Pay yaw pam *put* wikvaqa qa haqam.
Pay yaw nöömay aw nima.
145   Pay yaw tiimaya,
   pay yaw kivaq tangawtaqam.
    "Ta'ay,
    "aw kukuyva
    "hinpi hak soniwa."
150   Qa naanawakna,
   pu'sa mamqasya,
   pu' yaw pay wukotsu'a[t] pas yaw qa aw nönga.
Niq pay yaw itsivuti[t]
   pay yaw kivamiq kyaalay naayö'a,
155   pu' yaw kur pam qa loloma.

A'ne hovaq
   taataqt sosoyam pas yaw so'a,
     pu' yaw hikotaq'e
      pay pev sinmuy aw naayö'a.
160   Tiimayaqam hova'ikya[t]
   sosoyam so'a,
   sinom[u].
Pam naala wikvaqa,
   Lolenso,
165   *pam* kivayaqw aqw paki
   nöömay amum [nit] pu' yu'at [nit] pu' na'at àmumi paki.
Puma huur naa'utayaniqa'e
   qa so'a.
Pay yaw *puma* qa nönge'
170   pas yaw qavongvaqw pu' yaw puma nönga.
Pay yaw hak qa haqam,
   yaw kur sinom sosoyam so'a.
Pay yaw qa lomahinta.
Yaw wukotsu'a naat ev'e
175   pu' yaw *put* engem na'am paaholawu.
Engem paahota.
   "Hapi,
    "pay YAASANA."
Wuuhaq paahot yuku.
180   "IT um engem itanay wukotsu'at kiyat aw wikni."
Pu' pam put paahot enang put wukotsu'at kiyat aw tavito,
   pu' aw haawi.
   "Ta'ay,
    "nu ung ukiy aw wikni."
185   "Ta'ay,
    "pay pi nu nösha.
   "Um nuy oovi piw iikwiwtani."
   "Owi,
    "pay nu so'on ung qa piw iikwiwtani."
190   Pu' iikwita.
Kiyat aw'i.
Pitu.
   "Ta'ay,

"um YEV HAQAM haalaykyangw
195   "qatuni.
"IT nu YEV ungem kiva."
"Kwakawhay
"put uma inungem IT yukuya"
"IT nu pas naawakna," yaw aw lavayti."
200   Nit pu' angqw nima[t]
yaw kiy ev pituq
pay sòsoyam sinom yaw qa hin qatsi.
"Uma pay yuuyuwsiyani.
"Itam pay qa YEV yesni.
205   "Itam pay haqami YANGQW nöngakni."
Puma yuuyuwsiya.
Yuwsiyaq
pu' *puma* nönga.
Pantsatsq
210   nankwusa.
Pam Lolenso nöömay naavtiqa'e
pangqaq put amum nakwsu.
Pangqaq panwiskayngw
hoopokya Orayve öki.
215   *Pev* kitaqat kikmongwi aw öki.
"Itam umum YEV as yesni."
"Pu' uma haqaq PEW öki?"
"YANGQW taavangq Yungyatsayngaq itam öki.
"Itam oovi umum YEV yesni."
220   "Niq hiita uma aw YANKYAKYANGW
inumum YEV yesni?"
"Itam tsu'at,
"IT'A
"tiivaq
225   "yokvangwu,
"niq hakimuy uuyi'am lòlomatingwu."
"Antsa'ay,
"pay nu naawakna," kikmongwi kitaq
pay hu'wana.
230   Niq oovi *puma put amum* yeese.
Niqa'e oovi antsa tsu'tivangwu.

Niq antsa yaw a'ne yokvani.
Niq pay YAN HISAT oovi as put qa wunimangwu.
Puma ökiq
235   oovi put puma as *put* tiivangwu,
pumuy amutsviy,
pu' hapi *put* qa [naat] qa tiivangwu.

                          ▯

Yuk paasava.

LOLENSO

Long ago people lived at Yungyawsayvi.
And a certain beautiful girl there wanted no one.
The boys all desired her.
  The boys would come by,
5   but she wanted no one.
A homely lad there had only a grandmother,
  it is said.
He went to see the pretty girl on his own turn.
He got there
10   and she wanted him
and he married *her*.
The other boys got angry:
  they would take her away
    from the plain one.
15   "To take her away
    "we'll go hunting and
    "whoever bags the most rabbits will win her hand
      "this very evening."
So they all went hunting [and wagered that]
20   and the one who bagged the most would be the beauty's husband.
He [the homely one] won his own wife
  and they went off to his house
    and the boys got angry all over again
    [and so they said]
25   "We've got to take her away.
    "Way south at Grooved Mesa lives a rattler THIS LONG,
    he lives *over there.*

"So we have him fetch it

"and when he picks it up

30 "it'll kill *him.*

"And then we'll get into his wife."

So someone went along to tell him

and arrived at his house.

"Are you going around."

35 "I've come to give you the word."

"What is that?"

"You're to go get the big snake up at Grooved Mesa."

"And

"why is that?"

40 "You're to go get it so

"we can have a look at it

"to see what it looks like;

"no one has ever

"seen the likes of it."

45 "Okay,

"I'll go get it for you."

So off he went running

to bring the snake.

When he got to the edge of the mesa,

50 "Oh dear,

"can't help

"getting killed

"when I get there," he thought to himself.

He was going along thinking "poor me," when

55 from somewhere someone said,

"My grandson,

"where are you going?"

"Way up above HERE to get the big snake."

"Wait a minute.

60 "Come here."

He approached.

"Poor you,

"my grandson.

"He's always killing someone.

65 "You just take THIS with you," the voice said

and handed him some medicine.
"When you get there
"you put *it* in your mouth
"and when it gets mad at you,
70   "just squirt this ON IT.
"IN THIS WAY,
"you see,
"it won't get angry
"and will come to you."

▯

75   "What are you doing wandering about?"
"I've come to get you."
"Oh,
"is that so?"
"Over THERE IN YUNGAWTSAYVI kiva-goers,
80   *"they* want to look at you *in the worst way,*
"so they sent me.
"They wanted me to be the one to pick you up,
"so that's why I've come to bring you."
"For sure,
85   "I'll come with you;
"just wait here
"for me to get dressed."
So it went into its pit house
and went to the north wall
90   and picked a jar THIIIIS big
that held poison.
From this he drank.
And there was another
jar he picked up
95 and also drank from it.
He drank deeply.
"That will do it.
"let's go;
"they are waiting for you.
100 "You'll have to carry me on your back,
"being that I drank so much

"I'm heavy."
From there *he* carried *him* on his back.
Carried him north
105   and he was real heavy
and going *that way*
    they came to the village.
The big snake said,
    "Okay,
110   "go ahead and call out."
    So he shouted,
        "You all come here to relieve me of your father.
        "He's too heavy for me,
        "so come help me with the burden."
115   And so one of them went to the mesa edge to see
            who was yelling out.
Well, Big Snake was really rattling
just like a gourd rattle
    and they ran
120   and yelled into the kiva that
        Lolenso had COME BACK carrying Big Snake
        and it hadn't killed him.
They weren't happy;
they HUNG THEIR HEADS.
125   Many men were packed
into the kiva.
He brought it *to them*
    and announced,
        "HERE is THE ONE
130   "I brought HERE to you
        "so what do you all want me
        "to do WITH IT?"
No one said anything.
Those men were scared
135   and *he* set Big Snake down at the kiva
and it rattled so loud
    that *people* heard it.
        "Lolenso REALLY brought the Big Snake BACK HERE!"
        "Yes,

140   "let's go take a look."
           And along they came running.
     And it stood THIIIIS TALL!
     The one who brought it was nowhere.
     He had gone home to his wife.
145   People were looking on
     and someone hollered to those in the kiva,
     "Okay,
           "someone come out to have a look
           "and see what it's like."
150   The ones in the kiva didn't want to
     for they were scared shitless,
           and wouldn't come out for Big Snake
     who got mad
           and retched his poison into the kiva
155   and it must have been bad.
     It really stank and
           the men inside all died and
           the rest of the poison
     he vomited upon the people outside.
160   When the onlookers caught wind of it
     They all died,
           all of those people
     Only *the one* who brought the Snake,
           Lolenso,
165   had shut *himself* away in his pit house,
           having entered with his wife and her parents.
     They were shut tightly away
           and didn't die.
     It was not until
170   the next day that *they* emerged.
     Nowhere was there a soul.
     The people must have all died.
     It wasn't pretty.
     The Big Snake was still there,
175   so their father made prayer sticks *for it*.
     He made the prayer sticks for him [Lolenso].
           "There,

     76

"THIS IS ENOUGH."

He had made many prayer sticks.

180   "THIS you will take to the house of Big Snake."

He would take them back to Big Snake's house.

     And Lolenso climbed back down to the Snake.

"Okay,

     "I'll take you back to your house."

185   "You'll have to carry me again,

     "for I am indolent.

"Maybe you could carry me again."

"Yes,

     "I can surely carry you back."

190   And he put him back on his back.

They came to his home.

They arrived.

"Okay,

     "you go ahead and live HERE

195   "happily."

"I brought THIS HERE for you," [said Lolenso.]

"Thank you,

     "for making THIS for me.

"THIS IS WHAT I like," he said.

200   From there he came home.

And when he arrived at his abode,

     not a single person was left alive.

"We'll get ready.

"We can't live HERE.

205   "We will leave FROM HERE for somewhere else."

They got ready.

And when prepared for the journey,

     they left.

Having prepared that way,

210   they abandoned their home.

Lolenso got his wife back and

     from there they set out with *him.*

From there they went along and

     arrived eastward at Oraibi.

215   *There* they came to the village chief's house.

"We would like to live HERE with you."

"From where have you arrived HITHER?"

"From Yungyawtsayvi in the south we came HERE"

   "to live HERE with you."

220   "So what will you DO FOR A LIVING,

   "living HERE with me?"

"It is the Snake Dance,

   "THIS ONE,

     "when we dance it,

225   "it rains,

   "and everyone's crops come out well."

"Very well,

   that's what I want," the village chief said,

     agreeing to let them settle.

230   So *they* lived *there with him*

   and did the Snake Dance

   and it would really rain.

(But FOR SOME TIME *it* has not been danced.)

When they came

235   they danced *it*

   for them.

But now they don't dance *it* any more.

𝍥

That's as far as it goes.

Before discussing versification in the preceding narrative, we will con-sider sectionality and the narrative functions.

The story falls into four sections, based on change of scene/location: lines 1–31, 32–74, 75–189, and 190 to the end. The narrator uses actual mention (proper names, place-names, remention of a noun such as "the certain girl" or "the boys" or "the men") instead of proximal deictics to establish sections, reserving proximal reference for highlighting the action from line 120 to line 141. This is the part of the story that introduces the Realization function and that presages the destruction to come through casual dabbling with the supernatural. The sections are as follows:

  I   **setting/desire:** a certain girl will marry no one; a homely fellow, Lolenso, wins her hand; the other boys want to take her away, so they plan to send Lolenso off to get Big Snake.

II   **plan/journey:** Lolenso is dispatched to fetch Big Snake; Spider Woman gives him some medicine on the way.

III   **journey/realization:** Big Snake agrees to go and drinks poison; they arrive at the village, and the curious come out to see the Snake, which sprays them with poison; they all die, save Lolenso and his household; they emerge from hiding, and prayer sticks are made for the snake.

IV   **coda** (formal ending): Lolenso and his group abandon their village and go to Oraibi, where they are admitted because they have the Snake Dance.

Although proximal deixis is used for highlighting (see also lines 26, 90, and 142 for its use as a local emphatic device), the number of sections delineated by the storyteller is four, as indicated by the narrative functions.

The quatrains defined by subordination are given in table 2.4. They concern: (a) Lolenso's trip away from home, when Spider Woman helps him to achieve his goal; (b) Big Snake's preparation; (c) Lolenso's appeal for men in the kiva to come out and help him with his burden; and (d) the sensation that Big Snake causes before he exterminates the villagers. The episodes where the survivors leave for Oraibi and Lolenso explains about the Snake Dance (lines 211–14, 222–25) are also cast as quatrains.

TABLE 2.4. QUATRAINS IN "LOLENSO"

lines	summary
15–18	The men plan to take Lolenso's wife.
50–53	L. has self-doubt.
62–65	Spider Woman gives him medicine
67–70	and tells him how to use it.
71–74	Spider Woman sums up.[a]
84–87	Big Snake gets ready.
88–91	It drinks poison.
113–16	He calls for them to relieve burden.[a]
119–22	News about Big Snake spreads.
129–32	L. calls into the kiva.[a]
138–41	People discuss the sight.[a]
156–59	Big Snake poisons the villagers.
163–66	L. and his wife's family are shut away.

| 211–14 | They leave for Oraibi. |
| 222–25 | L. explains the Snake Dance.[a] |

a. Speech by a character.

This example illustrates that quatrains defined by subordination are effectively used in narratives in Hopi storytelling traditions other than Third Mesa. There is no way of predicting exactly where quatrains will be used by a given narrator, but moments crucial to the plot (and perhaps also key quotes) are often cast in quatrain form.

3

ADDITIONAL EXAMPLES OF VERSIFICATION

VERSIFICATION OF LINES BY subordination into quatrains is not only a characteristic of traditional Hopi narratives; it may also appear in the New Testament translation. For example, the second half of John 18:3 states in the English text (King James Version) that Judas and the arresting mob "cometh thither with lanterns and torches and weapons" (the Greek text has "comes there with torches and lanterns and weapons"). Here is the Hopi translation of that text, with a literal translation into English:

>Noqw puma wìiqöhi'ywiskyangw
> kopitsoki'ywiskyangw
> tunipi'ywiskyàakyangw
>   put amum pangsoya.

❖

>So they, coming with lanterns,
> and coming with torches,
> and coming with weapons,
>   went there with him.

The Hopi translator has taken the single line in English and created a quatrain in Hopi, which is not the only possible Hopi translation. The following is also possible:

>Noqw puma wìiqöhit nit kopitsokit nit pu' tunipit enang

kivakyàakyangw
put amum pangsoya.

𝟕

And they bringing
lanterns and torches and weapons
came there with him.

While this particular line is not overly important in the passage in which
it occurs, this example is not an isolated one. Hopi narrative conventions,
whether applied to traditional or innovative material, include a tendency
to versify in quatrains of four subordinate lines.

Another striking example of the use of quatrains, here in a group of four,
is found in the following speech uttered to kachinas before they go home
after dancing all day in the village plaza; the text is that of the kiva exhibit
in the Museum of Northern Arizona. (Other conventions characterizing
this text, especially the use of *ta'ay*, 'all right,' are explored in chapter four.)
Once again, proximal deictics are indicated in capital letters. There are
no distals in the text, so this is rhetorically a single, extended introduction
to a piece of discourse that has no development (and hence no distals).

Ta'ay,
   hapi nu se'elhaqam PEWHAQAMI umuy tokiltoyna.
Noqw pay hapi aqw pituy.
Antsa ura uma taavok teevep itamuy tiitaptotay.
5   Noqw pay IMA MOMOYAM naat kur umuy kwangwa'iwyùngqe
   umumi pan naanawaknaqe
     pu' uma piw naanawaknaqw
     oovi nu umuy YUKIQ ikivay aqw pay haak tangatay.
Noq se'el pu' nu umuy piw nöngaknaqw
10   oovi itam piw pu' suup YEP taawanawit hinnumyay.
Noqw pay antsa pi nu' YUK HAQAMI piw umuy tokiltoyna,
   umuy maatapniqey
   niqw hapi aqw pituy.
Pay hapi tapikiq,
15   pay nu mangu'iy,
   noqw pay uma sonqe piw tuwat maamangu'ay.
Pay hapi sonqe ephaqam umuy umungum,

umunam,
    pu' umùunatkom sonqe tuwat umuy nuutayyungway.
20   Niikyangw uma ep ökiye'e,
        tuu'awvayaq'öy
          itamuy ookwatutwe'ey
            angqw paalay akw itamuy poptayaniy,
            angqw put akw itamumi ökiwtaniy
25   pu' itam pu' IMA sòosoy hìitu popkot hiihikwye'
          akw öqawi'yungwniy.
            Pu' piw IT ITAA'UYIY piw puma aw ökiwtaqöy
            puma hikwye'ey,
              naatukwsinayaq'öy,
30   itam itàakiy ang put o'ye'ey
            itam put noonove'
             itam akw naayesni'yyungwniy
Pay qatsi yeesiway.
Pay YAN HAQAM hìntaniy.
35 Ason nu' umuy yuwsinaqw
    pu' umayaniy.
Ta'ay,
    pay uma hàalaykyàakyangw
    aqw haqami ninmaniy.

▮

All right,
    earlier today I set a time for you HERE
and it has come.
Verily you entertained us all day yesterday.
5 And the women are still enthralled,
    praying to you so
      you also would pray and
        for the time being I will contain you HERE in my kiva.
Early this morning I took you into the village
10 and HERE all day we were going along.
So I have set a time for you HERE
    to release you
      and it has come.
It is evening

15   and I am tired
    and surely you also are tiring as well.
    So also your mothers,
      your fathers,
        and your children surely await you;
20   when you arrive
          with word,
            pity us
              with rain;
                come to us
25   so we and other creatures may drink
                  and grow strong;
                    and also come to OUR PLANTS
                  so they may also drink
                  that they may mature
30   to fill our homes
                    that we may eat
                    and go on living.
    Life will go on.
    So it will be HERE.
35   When you are ready,
      you
        then
          happily
          will go home.

The main body of the text is made up of a series of four quatrains (17–20, 21–24, 25–28, 29–32) that articulate the prayer message of the speaker; the ritually important number sixteen (the ideal multiple of four, the sacred number in Hopi culture) occurs as the total number of lines of these quatrains. Two other quatrains may be distinguished (5–8; 36–39), one at the very end of the text. Quatrains make up most of the text (about 70 percent). The text is constantly highlighted; thus the extended use of both proximals and quatrains.

Several issues remain to be resolved concerning quatrains in the performance of Hopi traditional literature. One is whether quatrains are more typical of extemporaneous than of memorized oral production. While all performances are extemporaneous to a degree, quatrains (like any predictable discourse property) may well occur as a stock device, expected in given contexts.

Quatrains of subordinate clauses do not seem to be typical of direct quotations in traditional narratives. Ritual speech, such as the example above, might be long enough to occur in quatrains, but ordinary speech would not be expected to occur in this form. Yet another function of quatrains might be that of summarizing or emphasis in some stories.

Another issue is whether four successive, nonsubordinated lines may constitute a quatrain. Four such lines preceded by and/or followed by subordinated quatrains, might be justified as a quatrain. If this additional kind of quatrain is in fact distinguishable, then an additional dimension of rhetorical force is available to the raconteur or orator.

Yet another issue awaiting further exploration is the possible use of triplets and couplets in Hopi traditional narratives and other genres. Such additional units of versification would be expected to have modifying, emphatic, contrastive, clarifying or other amending functions with respect to quatrains.

Finally, versification and proximal marking are typical of other extended examples of Hopi verbal art, with each type exhibiting its own genre signature(s). Thus, there exists a traditional Hopi rhetoric for sectioning longer discourses and gathering the lines hierarchically into an architecture, while at the same time distinguishing genres by the pervasive use of genre markers.

4

HELEN SEKAQUAPTEWA'S
"COYOTE AND THE WINNOWING BIRDS"
A Sample Analysis

"COYOTE AND THE WINNOWING BIRDS," as narrated by Helen Sekaquaptewa, is a traditional Hopi story (H. Sekaquaptewa 1978) based on a videotaped performance (Evers, ed. n.d.). The Hopi version and English translation offered here are based on an unpublished translation of the Hopi transcript of one of Mrs. Sekaquaptewa's daughters, Allison Lewis. The following analysis illustrates how Hopi narrative structure is embodied in an actual story and includes a discussion of prosodic information as well.

There are two previous published analyses: D. Hymes (1992) and Wiget (1987). Wiget used a Hopi transcript prepared by Allison Lewis, a daughter of Mrs. Sekaqupatewa's, to bring the English subtitles of the videotaped performance (H. Sekaquaptewa 1978) closer in alignment to the lines of the Hopi text. Hymes used the same Hopi transcript for his analysis. My Hopi text came from checking the existing Hopi transcript against the videotape. My text and analysis differ from Wiget's in that they are based on a closer reading of the original Hopi performance rather than on a secondary source. My approach differs from Hymes in that the Hopi text is more accurate, especially in the division of the text into lines. For example, lines 4–6 in my text are as follows.

4   niqw ayám pay TSIRÒOT piw yaw ang naavinta,
5   hal *puma* pay tuwat **sumiYANkyàakyangw**
6   puuyawnumyangwu

🔳

4   and along over there LITTLE BIRDS abounded,
5   and in their **usual way**
6   they'd fly about.

This material in Hymes's version appears as follows.

18   niqw
19   ayam
20   (space)
21   Pai tsiroot piw, YAW, ang navvinta, hal puma
22   pai tuwat sumiyankyaa
23   kyang puuyawnumyangwu.

Hymes is using the particle *pay* to define lines, assuming that it is always an initial particle. This, however, is not true; *pay* may occur after the first word of a line (with a different meaning). His consistent use of *pay* (and other particles) as solely initial elements creates divisions of the text into lines that are not permissible in Hopi grammar (for example, the *kyang* in his line 23 is part of the suffix-*kyàakyangw*, 'as [plural],' and cannot be separated from the suffix) and lines that are not always supported by the intonation of the videotaped performance.

Wiget's discussion (1987:312–28) of the narrator's expressive features (intonation, volume, pausing; all **paralinguistic** features) and gestural (**kinetic**) performance complements the reading given here. I differ from Wiget in that I distinguish only three pitch-volume levels (high/low vs. normal), and that I take audience feedback as a crucial structural element. My approach throws the main prosodic and grammatical factors that trigger audience response into relief.

The present analysis differs from the others in two ways. First, both Wiget and Hymes used an unpublished transcription of the performance, while I compared the same transcript with the spoken text on the videotaped performance to produce the document below. Second, I used both initial particles and clause-final conjunctive suffixes to distinguish the levels of subordination that indicate rhetorically significant quatrains, while Hymes used only initial particles for versification. Furthermore, I did not attempt to carry the analysis beyond the local rhetorical significance of versification as Hymes does (he finds four "acts" of four "scenes" each based on an architecture signaled by initial particles).

Mention should be made of four particles that often do appear at the beginning of a line. The particle *noqw* shifts focus (64) or marks a transition (112). It may also mark new information. It is not frequent in this text.

The particle *niqw* serves as a link between lines (28, 66), translating as 'and so/as well.' It may be given the intonation (and pausing) that defines a line; in this usage, it functions like *noqw* (76). In the combination *niqw pu'*, 'and finally,' it indicates the last of a series (93). It may also be used with another particle to mark predicate inversion (98, 144), a tactic too complex to consider here in detail.

The particle *pu'* gives a sense of ending and completion. It almost always occurs on lines following a previous verbal subordinate marker (see, for example, 8–15, 76–81, 90–94). It rarely occurs on its own as 'and so then' (127), introducing an additional part of a sequence or event.

The particle *pay*, 'well,' has neither a sense of continuation (as with *noqw* and *niqw*) nor a sense of addition or completion (as with *pu'*). It is neutral with respect to completion/continuation, and in conversational Hopi is the "default" particle: clauses or lines without an initial particle are awkward, so if no other particle applies, one may always use *pay* in preference to a "naked" clause beginning. Occasionally, *pay* may occur at the beginning of a subordinate line to imply hesitation (88) or inconsistency (97).

An important, noninitial particle that requires comment is *yaw*, the quotative ('they say/it is said that'). This occurs throughout the fabric of this and all other Hopi traditional narratives. It is the genre signature, because it is found in nearly every narrative line. Most lines that do not consist of a character's quoted speech include the quotative *yaw*. Exceptions are lines without predicates (examples include subjects, objects, or adverbials preposed or extraposed for rhetorical effect). *Yaw* does not appear in these, nor does it usually appear in subordinate clauses/lines. Examples of extraposition include lines 93–94, 57, 133, and 200; no examples of preposing occur in the text.

It is also possible for the intonation (with accompanying pausing) to define a line to be given to a clause part (usually the direct object) if there is a series.

122   "uma nuy angqw umùumasay,
123   "umùupöhöhöy maqayaqw

7

122   "give me some of your wing feathers,
123   "and some of your downs

There is an extended example of this in lines 180 to 183. One must thus consider for just how many clauses a single *yaw* "lasts" (the domain of each use of the quotative).

In addition, the quotative *yaw* can be used to introduce an extended quote (an example is in lines 120 to 124), or a story song (32, 146). In such cases, *yaw* (or *pu' yaw*) has line intonation. Not all instances of the story song have this feature, however.

Deictically defined sections are based on proximally marked verbs and adverbs; noun topics ("birds," "Coyote") are established by use of the appropriate noun without any deictic marking; subsequent marking, however, is distal, as expected, with both "birds" and "Coyote" being rementioned.

The first section realizes the Setting function. (Proximals capitalized, and distals are in italics.)

7   the birds were harvesting . . .
15   picking seeds THIS WAY . . .
17   then getting together THIS WAY . . .
39   DOING THIS [singing while winnowing] . . .
53   they were DOING THIS . . .

In this section, a topic chain of four verbs describes the birds' actions, without mention of "flying," an action typical of birds and crucial in the story. The second deictically defined section begins with Coyote's Journey and subsequent Desire.

54   when COYOTE climbed up (the mesa) . . .
61   and he watched them secretly . . .
64   as they *did that* . . .
66   he had been looking for something to eat . . .
70   and thought . . .
72   "if I get THESE FEW ONES . . .
74   thinking THIS WAY . . .
      [and starts for them] . . .

The third section embodies the Plan function. There are in fact two plans here: one is Coyote's and the other is the birds'.

82	"I won't do anything to you . . .
86	"may I join you? . . .
89	they looked at each other
90	(DOING LIKE THIS)

Coyote then joins them as they winnow and sing (fourth deictically defined section; Realization function).

106	[singing] THIS WAY
107	they gathered it up ALONG HERE
108	and flew upwards . . .
110	DOING IT THIS WAY
111	and descended

Coyote expresses disappointment at not being able to fly up to toss the seeds in the winnowing basket so the wind will blow out the chaff. The act of flying is coded as 'do that' (distal) the next two times (lines 113, 137), but the fourth time they fly with Coyote (each bird having donated feathers), and the action is coded with proximals (fifth section; Realization continues).

158	the fourth time . . .
170	they WENT THIS WAY
171	Coyote going THIS WAY with them

They all take back their feathers midair, in a sixth section that ends the Realization function.

184	as poor Coyote was DOING THIS,
185	and went tumbling head over heels
186	crashed somewhere below
187	and the poor thing died

In the coda, line 188 to line 197, the birds chide Coyote in an overt evaluation section, which is infrequent in Hopi traditional narratives.

There is little formal subsectional structuring other than patterns defined on the basis of subordination. There is no use of specifiers, and there are only two obvious sets of parallel synonyms at the beginning of the story emphasizing the topic of the "seeds" that the birds are collecting (lines 6–7, 16).

There are four extraposed constituents (lines 57, 94, 133, 200), where the usual SOV (Subject-Object-Verb) order is disregarded. The first has the effect of highlighting the local setting (line 57). The next occurs when the birds' seeming agreement has convinced Coyote that his dinner plans are right on schedule (line 94). The third is encountered when the birds set up Coyote with the feathers (line 133), and the fourth (line 200) reports his literal downfall at the end of the story. Although there are only four extrapositions, they in essence frame the entire story. There are two other notable textual features that may more properly be thought of as intruding into the sectional structure: the story song and the frequent asides. These elements will be considered after a discussion of versification.

There are nine quatrains defined by subordination, the following seven:

42–45;
68–71;
78–81;
95–98;
116–19;
121–24;
183–86;

and four others to be discussed below. The first quatrain (lines 42–45) describes the process of winnowing step by step, leading up to the second instance of the story song. The second quatrain (68–71) recounts Coyote's arrival at his wish: upon climbing up, he spies the birds winnowing and thinks that "if I kill these few little ones, I'll eat nicely." The third quatrain (78–81) portrays Coyote's arrival at the ledge where the birds are actually winnowing.

> unable to restrain himself,
>   he set off to the birds,
>   and as soon as they saw him,
>   they wanted to run away

Each line moves the plot forward through a series of images of action. The fourth quatrain (95–98) describes Coyote's attempt to learn their song, concluding that "he didn't do it just exactly like them." The fifth and sixth quatrains (lines 116–19, 121–24) describes, in excruciating detail, Coyote's intense desire but inability to grab the little birds. Another quatrain (183–86) describes Coyote's inevitable fall.

> poor Coyote was going like this,
>   tumbling head over heels,
>   and crashed somewhere below,
>   and the poor thing died.

The giggles elicited from the audience in the videotaped original attest to the effectiveness of this quatrain. The two final lines of the last quatrain share a single quotative, where one is expected per line. By sharing a single quotative, these lines add to the cohesion of the quatrain. Such instances may be noted throughout the text.

There are two additional quatrains that are interrupted by asides (lines 127 . . . 131–32–33, 155–56 . . . 158–59). The interruption in the first case is a summary of the action; in the second case it is a reminder that this is the fourth time, so the climax of the story is nearing. These examples show that quatrains may be interrupted in an actual performance and still retain their force as quatrains.

Two other quatrains are formed by lengthening the long vowel (with its falling tone) of the word for 'birds' (lines 147–50, 165–68). Here Mrs. Sekaquaptewa ingeniously uses the falling tone of the word to (a) imitate the sound of the birds, (b) name them as a discourse topic capable of flight (as opposed to Coyote/Icarus who is not normally capable of it), and (c) iconically symbolize the main action of the story (gliding down from up in the air winnowing harvested seeds).

An almost cinematographic presentation of both action and motivation as a series of four lines is reflected by the four-fold repetition of the story song. The song itself describes the process of winnowing, one of four global story topics (the birds, Coyote, the winnowing process, and the birds' flight up on their last toss). The birds gather the seeds in their winnowing basket, circle around it, then fly upward as they gently toss the seeds and the breeze blows away the chaff. The fourth repetition of the song marks Coyote's ill-fated flight.

The song, occurring in four of the six deictically defined sections, serves to unify the story by increasing tension in the audience, who know that the fourth repetition of anything in Hopi culture will be significant. Coupled with the inherent irony of Coyote's mere presence, the results are inevitable. The known (and thus predictable) clues of narrative production foreground the predictable conclusion, but aesthetic tension is created only by the narrator's selectively varying the application of the standard narrative devices.

More directly related to the dynamics of performance (and less a part of narrative structure), asides are found at many more points in the narrative than the two interrupted quatrains mentioned above (lines 18–19, 33, 56–61, 65, 129–30, and 157). On the videotape, these asides always draw a reaction from the audience, and they are usually cast in a tone of voice similar to a stage aside or whisper. Asides usually allude to things that everyone in the audience can be presumed to know. Whether asides in Hopi traditional narratives function primarily to establish common presuppositions is a matter for further research.

Prosodic features nearly coincide with syntactic features. Syntactically defined lines almost always coincide with units based on sentential intonation and pausing; exceptions (other than the asides and audience feedback) are the four extrapositions. More important is the narrator's subtle use of volume (along with a slight increase in pitch) as a contrastive element: intonational contours and pausing are **regulatory mechanisms** in this performance that shape the flow and pace of the story, while volume (including pitch) is a **contrastive** (highlighting, foregrounding) **mechanism**.

The most noticeable feature of increased volume-pitch (hereafter, simply volume) is that the louder of the two registers transcribed almost always occurs at the end of lines. Since Hopi is a verb-final language, most of the highlights defined by volume are verbs; the actions (not the entities performing them) are the elements that propel the story onward. In the first part of the story (up to line 53), the only **volume topic** (a topic defined or marked by the use of volume) is the winnowing process. The repeated process of gathering the seeds together in the winnowing basket, tossing them in the air while singing the story song, and then on the fourth time flying upward while still winnowing is constant in terms of volume. 'Singing' (*tawlawu*) and the summary verbs ('do this way,' 'do that') are consistently highlighted. The products being winnowed (*tuusaqa*, 'grass' [line 8], *naapi'at*, 'chaff' [line 40]) and the instruments (*yungyaphòoya*, 'miniature winnowing baskets') are highlighted less frequently than the verbs, but are still prosodically related to the process.

After Coyote's chancing upon the scene (65), the winnowing process is marked by a distal reference (*pantsatskya*, 'do that way [pl. subject]'); the volume topic of the first deictic section ('winnowing') is rementioned with distal marking. Against this old information, Coyote's actions (mostly being hungry and looking around for food) are highlighted with increased volume. This leads to the volume climax of the piece (lines 77–81). It is here that Coyote's lack of self-restraint and its subsequent consequence is noted in the text (volume topicalization indicated by boldface type):

> and **unable to not show himself to them**
> **he set off straightway**
> **and as soon as they saw him**
> **they wanted to run away**

It is after this run-in that both Coyote's plan and the birds' plan begin to unfold in a series of Realization sections (III, IV, V; see the narrative, below) that increasingly build tension. It is significant that the volume climax of the piece includes the entire text of one of the quatrains (lines 78–81), giving further corroboration that the quatrains defined by subordination are a feature of traditional Hopi narrative practice, independent of the practice of any particular narrator.

In the Realization sections (lines 92–169, approximately 40 percent of the story), the winnowing process, Coyote, and the story song are the only topics highlighted with volume. The basic outline of the story has been established, and pausing in this section decreases. There is a brief interlude (lines 83–89), where Coyote approaches the birds and they agree to his participation, that is marked by a difference in volume topic. The next substantial use of contrasting volume (lines 177–84) occurs with a series of lines that are syntactically incomplete yet given sentential intonation:

177   they mobbed him and
178   back everyone's feathers came
179   from the wing
180   (they were) **plucked**
181   (from) **the tail,**
182   **the breast,**

183   **all of it** they plucked and
184   thennnn poor old Coyote DID LIKE THIS

If "plucked" is taken as a volume topic (with the two mentions counting as a single, synonymous unit), then the second volume topic highlights Coyote's desperate circumstances midair. Notably, the verb *yantsakma*, 'go along doing this way' (line 184), summarizes this volume quatrain and is itself highlighted with volume.

The last few instances of volume topicalization occur in the coda, where the birds speak to Coyote. They chide her/him (line 189 and following) and then resume doing what they were doing at the outset of the narrative: according to line 199 (which includes the last volume highlight **son oovi hiita puma qa**, 'so they must have'), 'so they must have continued conserving food for a long time.' The story ends shortly thereafter.

Other than the four instances of extraposition already considered, there is no other instance of disjunction of prosodic and syntactic marking other than the volume quatrain (lines 180 and so on). Following Woodbury (1987), mismatch between prosodic and syntactic cues is rhetorically significant, serving as a highlighting device.

It is the audience's contributions that test the reading proposed here: other than direct asides by the narrator to the audience, do purely textual or structural features function as cues for audience response to sustain the narrative? The most salient potential syntactic cues would be the deictically defined sections, quatrains outlined by successive subordination, and violations of the usual SOV word order. Since pausing and intonation contours are essential to defining prosodic lines (which coincide almost perfectly with syntactically defined lines), the primary potential prosodic cue would be volume highlighting, which most often occurs at the ends of lines.

Does audience response always occur after a shift to high volume register? In most cases (after lines 7, 22, 40, 63, 94, 171), audience response does follow increased volume. In the cases where the feedback is not immediate (after lines 54, 117, 187), the response is delayed by subordinated lines, suggesting that a series of such lines is a real cue to Hopi listeners. Two exceptions (audience feedback after no increase in volume), which occur after lines 105 and 142, are just after the third and fourth instances of the story song; by the third instance, the audience is interested in the song because they know the fourth time the song comes up it will be

95

significant (this is just before Coyote's fatal flight) and because they know that songs (even in text worlds) bring about a physical manifestation. Two further exceptions occur after lines 125 and 201; in line 125 the birds agree to feather Coyote and take him along on the flight portion of their winnowing song (a crucial point in the plot, perhaps marked by gestural or visual audience response), and line 201 is the end of the story (a very likely place for audience response).

Audience response to the narrator coincides neatly with the beginning of sections marked by proximals (after lines 54 [the beginning of II, the entrance of Coyote], 90–93 [a volume quatrain beginning the third section], 105 [IV], 162 [V], and 178 [VI; response delayed by subordination]). When a syntactically defined quatrain is highlighted with high volume, audience response also occurs (lines 90–93). Other instances of subordinated lines forming quatrains may be marked by gestural and/or visual responses, but it is notable that the only instance in this performance of verbal response to a quatrain occurred when the quatrain was highlighted by increased volume. The extended volume quatrain (lines 177–84, with summary line in 185) that marks the death of Coyote also initiates a verbal response.

Several structural features appear to serve as cues for verbal audience response to the narrator. Subordination is significant in defining quatrains, which, when highlighted with increased volume, will initiate a response. Subordination that is not itself emphasized may delay verbal response to preceding highlighted lines. The beginnings of deictically defined sections are always marked with loud register, and always receive verbal response. Deviations from Hopi SOV word order also trigger verbal response. The prosodic cue of increased volume (with an increase in pitch) is more salient than the syntactic cues, but both do serve to condition the audience's verbal feedback, particularly when there is a slight overlap. Other factors (the power of song as verbalization to bring about physical manifestation, the crucial quality of outcomes on the fourth repetition of something, the story cast as a journey that neatly matches the deictic sectioning) are less a matter of language use and more a matter of cultural relevance, but they all serve as cues to invite the audience's verbal response.

I have suggested possible ways in which a Hopi audience might determine when to respond to a storyteller performing a traditional Hopi narrative, first by considering possible syntactic cues and then by demonstrating the significance of these syntactic cues by considering interacting prosodic factors in an actual performance. Given the conventional use of the syntactic cues in the numerous flat texts in Hopi of Hopi traditional narratives, it is reasonable to expect that the use of loud register would be similar in other actual performances.

I have also shown that there are conventional means by which Hopis sustain interactive narrative performances. These conventions are to some degree idiosyncratic of Hopi culture, defining a genre. In addition to characterizing a traditional discursive practice in Hopi culture, however, most of these cues rely on the universal tendency to exploit the convenience of binary marking (the use of only two of the degrees of distance to mark sections that realize the Hopi narrative schema; the use of subordination as opposed to main clauses in versifying the text; the use of prosodic and syntactic junction or disjunction to mark rhetorically significant points; the use of two registers of volume and pitch to mark most points for the audience's verbal reaction; the use of a uniform intonation contour and rigid word order to delineate lines). Other cultural cues (the potency of songs, the power of four repetitions, the journey metaphor of any series of events worthy of casting as a story, the audience's response of *owi* or *oo*, 'yes') are integrated with the binary cues to achieve a rich narrative fabric.

THE TEXT

In the following text, a line is, as usual, defined as ending in a verb or nonverb predicate. In addition, the syntactic line nearly always coincides with an intonational unit (sentential intonation). Preposed and extraposed constituents of a single clause are treated as separate lines; fronted and extraposed constituents always carry sentential intonation. Relative clauses are considered to be part of the clause in which they are embedded, but subordinated clauses are indented after the independent clause they follow; successive subordinate clauses result in successive indentation. Asides to the audience, audience feedback, and appositives are set off in the text by centering. Audience response is not counted in the line numbering. Characters' speech is identified by quotation marks; audience feedback is prefaced by the notation "Audience:"; and asides and appositives are bracketed with parentheses. Boldface type has been used for higher volume-pitch level (loud register); upper case is used for proximal marking; and remention with distals is indicated by italics. Pauses are shown by ellipses; this does not indicate that material has been left out.

97

"TISAW NIQW PU' TSIRÒOT"

Diane: Itàaso, um as itamumi tuutuwutsi?
Helen: Ta'a.
Aliksa'i.
"Oo" uma kitota.
Aliksa'i.
Uma qa hingqaqwa.
Audience: Owi, owi . . .
Helen: Taq pi tuutuwutsi'ytaqa qövisaningwu,
hakim qa hu'watoynayaqw
    pay qöviste'
    qa tuutuwutsi.

☒

Audience: wi

☒

yaw **Oray**ve yeesiwa.
I   pay sinom pep pi yaw yeesiwa,
niqw ayám pay TSIROOT piw yaw ang naavinta,
hal *puma* pay tuwat **sumiYANkyàakyangw**
5   puyawnumyangwu.
pay *puma* tuwat tömöngmiq hoytaqw
    hìita nösiwqat **na'sastotangwu,**

☒

Audience: owi . . . 'wi

☒

nìiqe oovi hiihìita **tuusaqat** yaw **tukwsiqw**
    pu' *puma* pang kiy atkye'e,
10   pu' pay piw hikis oova pi pay tuuwi'ytaqw
pang himu pay hikis hin'ur **wungwngwu** niqw,
    put poosi'at **tukwsiqw**
        pu' yaw *puma put* ang ayám mawtinumyangwu,
yungyaphòoyat yaw himu'yyùngqe
15   *put* yaw YAN mawtotangwu.
Ang *put sivoshumiyat, poshumiyat* wuuhaqtote'

pu' yaw *puma* suuvo tsovaltotingwu,

𝄐

(haqam nen pu' yaw YAN, umun qönikiwkyàakyangw yesvangwu)

𝄐

20   pu' *puma* *put* yaw ep pi ini'yyùngqe
      put ep maamapriyaqw
       pam **pingngwu,**

𝄐

Audience: owi . . . 'wi

𝄐

pu' yaw *puma* *put* sòosoyam YAN yùngqw
   yaw *puma* **tawkyàakyangngw**
25   *put* wuhitotangwu.
   yaw **pay pi tumala'ytaqw**
   maqsoni,
   niqw oovi pay yaw *puma* **tawkyàakyangw**

30   oovi yaw sòosoyam ang **yesve'**
      pu' yaw **tawlalwangwu,**
   yaw,

𝄐

(put pay uma sonqe taawi'yyungwa)

𝄐

      pota pota poota,
35   pota pota poota,
      yowa'ini,
      yowa'ini,
      pu', pu', pu', pu'.

𝄐

yaw **YANTSAKLALWAQW**

40   pu' yaw ang **naapi'at** ayó' **puuyaltotingwu,**

◪

Audience: 'wi . . .

◪

hoytaqw
  pu' yaw hìita aw o'yat
  pu' yaw piw peehut ang **tsovalaye'**
  piw *put* piingyayat
45   pu' yaw **piwyangwu,**
teevep *puma pantsatskyaqe*
pi ep **tawlalwangwu,**

◪

    pota pota poota,
    pota pota poota,
50   yowa'ini,
    yowa'ini,
    pu', pu', pu', pu'.

◪

yaw *puma* **pantsatslalwaqw**
II   yaw kur **Iisaw** angqw taavangöyngahaqaqw wuuvi,

Audience: 'wi . . .

◪

55   nìiqe yaw pep Orayvi wuko'owa.

◪

    (uma put qa tuwi'yyungwa,
    Orayvit[a]?
    pam hapi Orayvi,
    pep wuko'owa **YANTA,**
60   aa village aa,
    kiihut taavangqöyve)

◪

pangqaqw yaw kur *pam* na'uy'kyangw
amumi **tayta,**

◪

Audience: um . . . um . . .

◪

noq *puma* **pantsaklalwaqw**

◪

65   (pay pi puma hìitu sutsep tsöngmokiwnumyangwu)

◪

niqw pay kya pi as *pam* **kwayngavo** hìita pay **hepto,**
pay pi **hìita** öö'öqat pi pay sinom maspitotangwu.
niqw put yaw *pam* heptoqe
oovi aw **wupqw**
70   yaw *puma pep* **pantsatskyaqw**
yaw *pam* wuuwanta,

◪

"is as nu' IMUY HIISA'NIQAMUY qöye'
kwangwanösni."

◪

yaw **YAN** wuuwankyangw
75   amumi **tayta.**

◪

Audience: 'wi

◪

niqw,
pay yaw as oovi qa **amumi namtsiknat**
pu' pas qa na'angwu'y[ta]qe

pu' yaw amumi nakwsuqw
80   yaw tutwaqe
pu' yaw pay as watqani.

𝟐

"nu' pay son umuy **hintsanani**,"

𝟐

yaw amumi kita,

𝟐

"pas hapi uma sosonkiwyaqw
85   oovi nu' angqw umumi nakwsu;
ya sen' son **umumumni**?"

𝟐

yaw amumi kitaqw
pay yaw . . . yaw naanami **yoyrikya**.

𝟐

III   (YANTOTI)

𝟐

90 pay yaw sòosoyam sumataq **naanakwhaqw**
pu' yaw pi oovi amumum **qatuptuqw**
pu' yaw pay oovi aw **yungyap**toynaya,
niqw pu' yaw oovi nùutum *pantsaklawu*,
pep pam'i.

𝟐

Audience: um . . . 'wi

𝟐

95 yaw piw oovi aw **intotaqe**
piw naat **tawlalwaqw**
pay pi *Iisaw* naat pu'niqw
taawi'yta yaw niqw,

pay oovi qa su'amun kya pi pay **YANTSAKNI**.
100   piw tawlalwaqe

🮱

pota pota poota,
pota pota poota
yowa'ini,
yowa'ini,
105   pu', pu', pu', pu'.

🮱

Audience: [naaniya]

🮱

IV   ep YANTOTIT
pu' yaw ang himuy YANG **o'yat**
pu' yaw **puuyaltotingwu,**
oomiq haqami,
110   hìisavo yaw angqe YANNUMYAT
pu' piw hanngwu.
noq *Iisaw* pi qa hìita masa'ytangwu,
nìiqe pay yaw okiw *pantotiqw*
qa nùutum puuyaltiqe
115   amumiq yaw YAN tayta,
pay pi **haqtotiqw**
kur hin pu' ngu'ataniqe

🮱

Audience: 'wi

🮱

noqw pay piw hanqe
piw naat antotiqw
120   pu' yaw
"sen . . . nu' . . . sen son
"uma nuy angqw umùumasay,
"umùupöhöy maqayaqw

"sen nu' umumum puuyaltini,"

◫

125   amumi kitaqw

◫

Audience: 'wi

◫

pay yaw sunanakwha.
pu' yaw hak oovi

◫

(*puma tsiròot* himuy naapa tsotspilalwakyangw
130   pu' yaw *Iisawuy haqami*)

◫

hak masay tsoope'
pangso' tur yaw ang put tsurumnaya,
    Iisawuy ang'a.
paas yaw oovi aptsinayat
135   pu' yaw piwya,
piw aw intotaqe
pu' yaw piw *pantsatskya,*

◫

pota pota poota,
pota pota poota,
140   yowa'ini,
yowa'ini,
pu', pu', pu', pu'.

◫

Audience: Ya sen Iisaw tsoni'yta?

◫

tsoni'yta yaw nùutum,
pay yaw pi **suutaw'yva** yaw nìiqe [oovi'o].

145 pu' yaw oovi ang o'yat
 pu' yaw

     🔲

  "tsiirò

   ò

    ò

150   ò
 yaw kitotat
  pu' oomiq pu'
 pay hapi yaw *Iisaw* nùutum puuyalti.
 pay yaw oovi qa **suus** amumum puuyaltit
155 pu' piwyaqw
  yaw **nùutungk**

     🔲

  (**hal** pay kya naalös haqamtotaqw)

     🔲

  naalösni'ywisqw
  pu' yaw *puma tsiròot* naami na'uyhìngqaqwa,

     🔲

160   "pu' hapi aw pitu,"

     🔲

  yaw kitota,

     🔲

 Helen: [naani]

     🔲

 pu' yaw oovi *puma* piwya,
 piw *pàntotiqe*
  piw yaw aqwhaqami

     🔲

165   "tsiirò

    ò

    ò

    òt

   kitotat

V 170 angqe YANNUMYAQW

   Iisaw yaw nùutum **YANNUMA.**

        🔲

Audience: [naaniya]

        🔲

pu' yaw *tsiròot* sumitsvoaltiqe

naami [yu'a'atota],

        🔲

"ta'a tuma,

 175 aw pitu,"

        🔲

yaw kitotaqw

pu' yaw aw homikmaqw

hak hìita himuy yaw angqw **tsoopangwu,**

masay hak maqe'

 180 put **tsoopangwu,**

   suruy,

   pöhöy,

   sòosok yaw ang tsotspitotaqw

VI pu' yaw okiw *Iisaw* angaqw **YANTSAKMA,**

 185 namtötötimakyangw

   atkyamiq haqam yeevaqe

   yaw okiw mooki.

        🔲

Audience: [naaniya]

        🔲

yaw hànqe

puma aw **tsùyti,**

▮

190   "**pay pi naap** uu'unangwayniq'ö,
naapas himu hin itamuy
um as sowaniqey wuuwankyangw
YEP itamumi pitu,"

▮

yaw aw kitotaqw

▮

195   "oovi pay itam ung niinayaqw
pay itamuy qa sowani,"

▮

yaw aw kitota.
pu' yaw àapiy *puma* naanalt *pantsaklalwa*,
pay yaw **son oovi hìita** *puma* **qa** wuuhaq tunösna'satota,
200   *pep taawat ep'e.*

▮

pay YUK pölö.

"COYOTE AND THE WINNOWING BIRDS"
Diane: Our grandmother, will you tell us a story?
Helen: Okay.
Harken.
  You all say "yes."
Harken.
  You're not saying anything—
Audience: Yes, yes . . .
Helen: Recall that storytellers are fussy,
  and if no one answers back,
    she'll get annoyed
      and then she'll quit.
Audience: Uh-huh.
Helen: They were living at **Oraibi**.
I   People were living there,

and along over there LITTLE BIRDS abounded,
and in their **usual way**
5   they'd fly about.
Well when it got along towards winter,
they would **store food away,**

◩

Audience: yes . . . uh-huh

◩

And so all kinds of **grasses grew there**
and *they*, going around below their abode,
10   (from) where there was a ledge higher up
things really **grew in abundance**.
that grass was really thick and
they would go up there *to pick it,*
equipped with tiny **winnowing baskets**.
15   They'd pick *it* THIS WAY.
Along where *the seeds* were prolific
they would assemble in a spot,

◩

(They'd be THIS WAY, in a circle
like you're sitting.)

◩

20   *They* would put *it* in,
rub *it,*
crunch *it,*

◩

Audience: Yes . . . uh-huh

◩

They would all move their plaques LIKE THIS,
and *they* **sang**
25   as (they) winnowed.

Well their **work,**
  was drudgery,
and so *they* **would sing**
  to break up the monotony.
30 So there *they all* **sat**
  and (they'd) **sing**
  it is said

𝈬

(I suppose you know this song)

𝈬

      pota pota poota,
35   pota pota poota,
      yowa'ini,
      yowa'ini,
      pu', pu', pu', pu'.

𝈬

  as (they) DID THIS
40 then **the chaff** would just **fly away.**

𝈬

Audience: uh-huh . . .

𝈬

So it went and
  they would put in some more and then
    around the remainder (they'd) **gather**
    and after **crushing** *it,*
45   (they'd) **do it again,**
and all day long *they did that,*
  singing
      pota pota poota,
      pota pota poota,
50   yowa'ini,
      yowa'ini,

pu', pu', pu', pu'.

█

So *they did it like that* and
II   it seems as if **Coyote** had climbed up the south edge,

█

Audience: uh-huh . . .

█

55   of the big rock of Oraibi

█

(You all know
Oraibi?
Oraibi is
the boulder over there **LIKE THIS**
60   on—uh—
the south side of the village.)

█

From there *he* had concealed himself and
on them (he) **fixated,**

█

Audience: Uh-huh . . .

█

and so *they were doing this*

█

65   (Those critters are always looking for food.)

█

and so *he* probably **cased the dump** for something,
something like the bones people throw away.
So as *he* was looking around

he chanced to **climb up** and
70   as *they were doing that there*
he got to thinking

◪

    "If I kill THEM LITTLE THINGS,
    I'll really pig out."

◪

He was thinking **like THIS** as
75   (he) **watched** 'em.

◪

Audience: Yeah.

◪

So
(he) hadn't **shown himself to them**
but he just couldn't control himself
so he set out towards them and
80   **as soon as (they) saw him**
    (they) wanted to run away.
      "I'm not gonna **do anything** to yuh,"

◪

he told them,

◪

    "You're really fascinating to watch and
85   that's why I came over to you;
      can I **join with you?**"

◪

he said to them and,
    well, they really **looked** at each other

◪

III   (LIKE THIS)

〽

90   and they all seemed **to agree** and
     then he sat down with them and
       they gave him a winnowing basket,
     and so he *did that* with them,
      he really did.

〽

Audience: mmm . . . uh-huh

〽

95   So again (they) **put it in** and then
     (they) still **sang** and
       Coyote still
         did not have the song down so
          that's why he didn't quite **DO IT LIKE THIS**.
100   So again they sang

〽

       pota pota poota,
       pota pota poota,
       yowa'ini,
       yowa'ini,
105   pu', pu', pu', pu'.

〽

Audience: [laughs]

〽

IV   and after DOING THIS,
     ALONG HERE (they) **set down** their stuff
     and would **fly**
   upwards somewhere,
110   for some time (they'd) DO THIS and then
     down they would come.
     Coyote was clean out of wings,

so the poor thing *couldn't do that* and
didn't fly with the others but just
115   longingly **looked** at them LIKE THIS;
having **gone so far up**,
   he couldn't nab 'em and so

🜚

Audience: yeah . . .

🜚

so when (they) got back down
(they)'d do it all over again
120   aaaand

🜚

"Say, . . . couldn't you
   give me some of your wing feathers
     and some downs
       so as I could fly with yuh?"

🜚

125   he said to them and

🜚

Audience: yeah . . .

🜚

(they) readily agreed.
So each

🜚

   (*Those birds*
   plucked themselves silly
130   and *on Coyote*)

🜚

from wherever they had plucked a feather
   there (they) would stick it in

on Coyote.
So after they had covered him enough
135   they went at it again,
again (they) filled and
again (they) *did that*, [singing]

🎵

pota pota poota,
pota pota poota,
140   yowa'ini,
yowa'ini,
pu', pu', pu', pu'.

🎵

Audience: So Coyote really got off on that?

🎵

(He) was so thrilled to be with them that
he **picked up on the song**.
145   So after they set down their baskets
and said

🎵

"Biii
ii
ii
150   irds,"
they say that
way up
with them flew *Coyote*.
And (he) didn't fly with them **just once**:
155   (they did it) again and
(he went **after them**

🎵

(**Recall** this is the fourth time.)

🎵

114

and on the fourth time
   then *those birds* said secretly
160   "The time has come,"

◪

they said,

◪

Helen: [laughs]
so again *they*
   did that and then
      they went even higher and it was

◪

165   "Biii
        ii
        ii
          iirds"

◪

that they said and then
V 170   as they WERE GOING AROUND LIKE THIS
      Coyote **WAS GOING ABOUT LIKE THIS** with them

◪

Audience: [laughs]

◪

and *the birds* bunched up and
   said
      "Okay,
175   time's up,"

◪

so they say and
   they mobbed him and
      back everyone's feathers **came,**
from the wing

180   (they were) **plucked,**
       (from) **the tail,**
          the breast,
       all of it they plucked and
VI   **and thennnnn** poor *old Coyote* DID LIKE THIS,
185   turning head over heels as
                downward somewheres he crashed and
                the poor thing died.

                        ▊

Audience: [laughs]

                        ▊

So (they) came down and
   they **derided** him:

                        ▊

190   "It's your own damned fault;
          it was with malice you,
          thinking of eating us,
             came HERE to us"

                        ▊

they said,

                        ▊

195   "So we killed you and
          you didn't get to eat us,"

                        ▊

they said.
So from then on, *they* had to *do it* by themselves,
and so *they* surely put away plenty of food,
200   *on that day.*

                        ▊

And THIS is where it ends.

Part 2

OTHER GENRES

DIRECT ADDRESS IS A heuristic label for a variety of discourse types that all involve a speaker addressing an audience. *Indirection* (the substitution of other words for 'you' for politeness) is typical of most of them. Typically, they are delivered in public by mature men. They differ from narration (*tuutuwutsi*) and singing (*tawlawu*) in not having a text that may be situated outside the moment or context of speaking.

In *tsa'alawu*, 'announcing,' limited *themes* (ideas) are repeated with formula beginnings and endings; they usually have a Rise-Hold-Fall (**RHF**) intonation contour at the end of lines, and especially at the end of an announcement. The beginning and ending formulas, and the RHF contour are genre signatures.

Proximal marking is used to identify topics in announcements, with longer examples having quatrains, couplets, and triplets defined syntactically by subordination. The lines are similar to those of narrations (usually a simple sentence with distinct intonation).

Public and private prayers (*unangwvàasi*) begin with the genre signature *ta'a*, 'already/okay.' Private prayers have no typical ending, while public prayers have the theme "go(ing) along happily" at the end. Prayers have a limited number of themes, but versification may be used to create internal architecture instead of defining sections by using proximal markers.

Like any language, Hopi has fixed expressions like English *thank you* and *good morning*. Some of the fixed expressions might be heuristically termed **sayings**; they have no Hopi name. Sayings are stock expressions a single sentence in length that address a particular action or situation. They may be humorous. Sayings do not have genre signatures.

Admonitions (*maqastutavo*, 'cautionary advice') do have genre signatures: they are intended for a particular action or situation. Like sayings, speakers of admonitions may be of either sex.

Because of the impact of western culture on Hopi life since 1900, Hopis make prepared speeches (*lavay'oyi*, 'layered language'). These use proximals and distals to define sections, as in narration, and also use subordination to versify lines into quatrains and other arrangements for rhetorical effect. *Lavay'oyi* do not typically use indirection, or beginning and ending formulas. I have termed this speechmaking as oration. Study of traditional oration, much of which is esoteric, is a topic for future research. In particular, the study of clown speeches could be an interesting avenue of research.

Mention should be made of Hopi jokes and humor. Often ironic and indirect, Hopi humor is found in a number of genres, as well as in conversation. Like traditional oration, Hopi humor and jokes are a topic for future research.

Hopis use the word *taawi* for both 'song' and 'songpoem.' Heuristically, the two may be distinguished from each other because songpoems are deliberately composed for public events each year and this repertory is thus infinite and dynamic. Songs, however, are a part of folkloric or ritual tradition, and are thus finite in number. Moreover, songpoems are structurally more complex, and have a standard form which is their genre signature.

Songpoems are composed, redacted in a group, and performed by men. Story songs (which are part of a traditional narrative) and ritual songs are performed by either gender, and children's songs by both girls and boys. Lullabies and grinding songs are sung by women. Songpoems that are especially memorable may be sung by men while working, especially in the field. I am not aware if women sing songpoems to themselves; indeed, the role of women in Hopi musicmaking remains to be studied.

5

DIRECT ADDRESS GENRES AND INDIRECTION

IN THIS CHAPTER, several direct address genres will be considered: *tsa'alawu*, 'public announcements/chants,' prayers, proverbs, sayings, and orations. All have distinct properties and/or genre signatures, and all theoretically interact with a Hopi principle of indirection. The longer direct address genres (some *tsa'alawu*, orations, and possibly longer prayers) utilize certain features of such longer genres as traditional narratives, specifically the deictically defined sections and a tendency to group chains of subordinate clauses into rhetorically significant quatrains. In direct address genres, intonationally defined lines tend to correlate with syntactically defined lines. The combination of this correspondence and the principle of indirection provide a commonality among direct address genres that makes them more similar to each other than to other Hopi traditional genres. Indirection is also employed in Hopi conversation, but I will show that conversation is distinct from direct address genres.

TSA'ALAWU: PUBLIC ANNOUNCEMENTS
The Hopi genre known as *tsa'alawu* is often called 'chant,' although "public announcement" is more accurate. Announcements/chants are performed on the roof of a building or the highest available place, usually in the morning (especially at sunrise), year-round, and can be secular or ceremonial. Sometimes a chant is given the evening before an event. Ceremonial chants are a part of the ritual process and consist of an audible part addressed to the town and a second, inaudible part addressed to supernaturals. Ceremonial chants are performed by the

tsa'akmongwi, an official 'crier,' who holds a priestly office assigned to a particular clan.

Secular chants may be performed by any adult male who knows the traditional style. Made on behalf of another party, they concern grievances, trading, wedding and naming feasts, work parties and bees, cleaning of communal areas, communal hunts, social dances, and the like. A second party announces for an individual or household, as it is considered rude or pushy to publicize one's own civic affair.

The first paper on this topic (Voegelin and Euler 1957) differentiates *tsa'alawu* from normal speech; it also suggests that there are dialect differences in *tsa'alawu*, just as there are such differences in speech. Voegelin and Euler observe that the content (as basic types of information, or **themes**) is limited, and that what is distinctive about the genre is the way its typically limited information content is distributed. They point out that the basic unit of *tsa'alawu* is a paragraph delineated "by one of two inflections: a long tonal crescendo, with tone rising first and then falling— for chants addressed to Hopi listeners; a long intensity crescendo, with tone held at the same level addressed to the supernatural chiefs" (1957:117).

A *tsa'alawu* is performed in a somewhat shrill, prolonged monotone, with its rhythm dictated by the words. An announcement of a ceremony is usually delivered by the crier chief *(tsa'akmongwi)*; sometimes a member of a particular clan might make the announcement of the public aspect of the ceremony controlled by that clan. Secular *tsa'alawu* can be made by any mature male. It is primarily with secular *tsa'alawu* that the present chapter is concerned.

The central study of Hopi secular *tsa'alawu* is R. Black (1964), which summarizes the genre as follows:

> Hopi chanting is a form of non-casual verbal behavior with broad areas of selection restrictions: in the sequence of utterances made, in the stylized manner of the introduction and conclusion, as well as in the substantive portions of chants. This restriction is further illustrated by the repeated use of stereotyped phrases which accompany the chant message. (1964:xxxix)

The restricted nature of *tsa'alawu* (limited amount of information, stylized way of rendering it, genre signatures of beginning and ending formulas and stock phrases) readily shows how Hopi "prose" discourse is sectioned below the genre level. "In casual speech, information is not repeated as a rule, while in chanting the words and phrases of the message may be repeated several times" (R. Black 1964:xi). As will be seen below, the way these repetitions are handled is significant.

Black notes that the genre signature *yaahahà* often initiates secular *tsa'alawu*, although other openings are possible; often people are addressed generically ("girls and women," "boys and men") or even more collectively (*Hopisinom*, 'Hopi people'). Endings are also formulaic: "it is already like that" (*Pay yan haqamo*) or "we are going along happily" (*pay hàalaykyàakyango*), or some permutation of these (R. Black 1964:xxi; the Hopi text has been edited and new translations have been supplied). In a content analysis of eighty-one secular *tsa'alawu*, Black notes only a few types of information typically broadcast: time of activity, personnel, type of activity, itinerary, identity (of person requesting the chant, for example), rendezvous point (for hunts), affective references ("be happy"), dreaming (of a successful activity), source of information (in grievance chants; always indefinite), opportunities for courting, redress of grievances, deterrent, specification (goods to be traded, crops to be planted or harvested, animals or children causing damage to crops, etc.). These thematic foci, fleshed out by actual details, cluster into announcements for four major kinds of secular event: work or hunting parties, sociable activities [feasts], grievances [involving "polite reprimands"; R. Black 1964:xviii], and trading. Themes are appropriate to a specific message; thus an announcement of a communal hunt will specify a rendezvous point, itinerary, and type of game to be hunted, but omit grievance themes (polite reprimand, grievance, deterrent). Black published two accounts of Hopi secular announcements (1967a, 1967b), on hunting announcements and grievance announcements, respectively.

Arizona Tewas have a similar genre, the *túkhé*, 'carry the word' (Kroskrity 1992). This announcement genre uses intonational paragraphs (high pitch, falling contours at major junctures), addresses the audience as "men, boys, women, girls," and uses the ending "this is what I have told you." All of this is very similar to the Hopi genre. As will be seen below, longer *tsa'alawu* are sectional, like traditional narratives; Kroskrity's examples are brief, so there is no way of knowing if Tewa announcements may be textually elaborated (involving remention of a limited number of themes to build up a structure with narrative sections).

As ethnoliterature, the *tsa'alawu*, especially the grievance announce-ment, is "essential information [that] is embellished by the repetition of affective references — emotionally laden utterances which are consonant with the communal nature of Hopi life and which tend to generate pub-lic acceptance of a particular situation" (R. Black 1967b:57).

The key to this harmonic ideal is indirection: "A person finding a cause for complaint [for example] will usually approach an experienced chanter to ask him to announce the grievance" (R. Black 1967b:57). Grievance announcements touch the very fabric and ideal of Hopi culture; one does not attempt a grievance directly, on one's own; one gets a third party to do this. Making one's own announcement could "embarrass his listeners, since his efforts are likely to be unpleasant, performed rapidly and in a loud voice, with a tendency to break into falsetto. An experienced chanter would avoid the use of displeasingly aggressive vocal qualities" (R. Black 1967b:58). The use of indirection, very evident in other aspects of Hopi culture, is focal-ized in grievance *tsa'alawu*, which epitomize this feature of Hopi discourse.

In terms of length, the large sample of secular announcements in Black (1964) range from as few as two or three clauses of information in the body of the announcement to from ten to twenty clauses of information in larger examples. Black sections examples of the announcement genre by the rise-hold-fall (RHF) intonational ending, which is a signature of this genre. Internal sections are intonational contours ended by pauses; these smaller intonational units usually contain a linguistic phrase or clause. As will be seen below, there is also a syntactic method of sectioning public announce-ments that only partially corresponds to the prosodic marking, however.

Several interrelated points may be made about the phonology and gram-mar specific to secular announcements as reported by Black. In the first place, the vowel /i/ becomes /e/ (a lenis, midfront vowel), as in the fol-lowing examples, transcribed into the current orthography:

Oovi uma qa **hen** naanawaknat (1964:302)
"Don't be shy."
Ason pi pay **heyta** naanawakne' (1964:344)
"If you want anything"

In the first example, *hen,* 'thus,' appears instead of *hin;* in the second, *heyta,* 'something,' appears instead of *hìita.* In a similar way, *senom,* 'peo-ple,' appears for *sinom,* and *etam,* 'we,' for *itam* in numerous examples. Yet /i/ is preserved in postpositions (*itamumi*, 'to us,' not **etamumi*). This feature (/i/ to /e/ shift), which seems to be limited to stressable vowel positions, occurs in examples from all three dialect areas of Hopi in Black's data.

In the second place, the quotative particle *yaw* is used to indicate a future tense, with a strong intentional sense.

Qaavo **yaw** etam et itaanay
Itàangùy pumuy amungem hökwisaniqat (1964:269)
"Tomorrow we will harvest corn
for our fathers and mothers."
Nu' **yaw** imuy
Ayaalawneey
Momoyamuu, mamantuuy (1964:285)
"I will request that you women (and) girls"

Two other features common to *tsa'alawu* are lengthened vowels (*ayaalawu*, 'request,' in the example above, for *ayalawu*) and the **pausal** (a copy of the final vowel or appearance of an unpredicted final vowel; the pausal of *nöösa*, 'eat,' is *nöösa'a*; examples of added final vowels are: *momoyamuu* for *momoyam*; *mamantuu* for *mamant*). These features help to make announcements audible over a wide area.

A final feature is the use of the emphatic ending -*y*, which imparts a sense of urgency. It is used more by adult male speakers than others, and it is different from the objective case marker -*y* (example: *ima*, "these," objective form *imuy*). The emphatic -*y* adds a sense of urgency and solidarity to the announcement; it is likely to occur at the end of major intonational sections (those marked by the rise-hold-fall intonation pattern).

Thus there are a number of distinctive genre markings of the secular announcement: the rise-hold-fall intonational signature (RHF), pauses, vowel lengthening, pausals, a tendency to shift /i/ to /e/, the use of the emphatic utterance-final marker -*y*, and a peculiar use of the quotative *yaw*. Of these, the prosodic markers (RHF, pausing, vowel lengthening, pausal vowels) are the most characteristic and may be considered the principal genre signatures; the other markers are more sporadic, yet also typify the genre.

The essential features of secular announcements are found in the following short example. In the text, a backslash (\) is used to mark the RHF intonational pattern. Each intonationally separate line (whether clause or phrase) is separated by an RHF or a pause. Where there is no RHF, a pause occurs at the end of the line to separate it from other lines. Where there is an RHF, the final vowel has also been lengthened with falling tone (shown by a grave accent).

Kur piw peqw tuqayvastota huvamùuy\
Pangqey kya uma sinom sòosoyam talahoyàay\
Uma yaw yukyiq
  hakiy kiyat aqw sòosoyam nöswisnìiy\
Oovi uma qa hin naanawaknat sòosoyam aqw nöswisnìiy\
Pay hàalaykyàakyangòoy\

*

Maybe again all of you will listen:
Around here, you people, as soon as it gets light,
You here
  will go to eat at so-and-so's house.
So don't be shy and all (of you) go to eat.
(We are) going along happily.

This announcement was supplied by Emory Sekaquaptewa; the translation is my own.

Other traditional direct-address genres of Native American cultures in the Southwest resemble Hopi *tsa'alawu* in consisting to a large extent of a limited number of culturally relevant themes and formulaic expressions (with or without parallelism). Piman ritual oratory, for example, tells the story of a mythological hero's journey that is specific to a particular occasion (war, salt gathering expedition, etc.; Bahr 1975:5). These orations contain often repeated "journey words" (1975:14–15), and the structure of the narrative consists of expanding a base sentence of the episode through parallel repetitions (1975:16–21).

The limited thematic nature of southwestern direct-address genres is striking. For example, the English translation of a speech by the governor of Laguna Pueblo on the village's saint's day (Goldfrank 1923:193) contains the following themes:

be good/honest
go ahead (and do) [the dance for the saint]

(references to good health)
(references to fertility)

These account for most of the information conveyed in the translated text. By sharing common themes and formulaic expressions, a seemingly isolated text or performance of an announcement or oration is related to other (actual and potential) examples of the same type (**intertextuality**). The same feeling of relatedness is also created by genre signatures. Common themes, formulaic expressions (especially beginning and ending formulas), and genre signatures culturally validate actual performances of a genre. The use of a limited number of prosodically highlighted themes makes form as important as (if not more important than) content.

This feature is also typical of limited-thematic, direct-address genres outside indigenous southwestern cultures. For example, chanted sermons of American Black folk preachers carry a limited amount of information (Rosenberg 1970). Although more musical than *tsa'alawu* (they are delivered following a pentatonic scale; 1970:17) and metrical (there is a basic metrical unit realized by a variety of rhythmic figures; 1970:38–39), this tradition also uses certain formulas to validate a given performance as a bona fide example of the genre: "The preacher relies on stock phrases and passages to fill out the skeleton of the sermon, and develop the message through repetition" (1970:31). It is the rhythmic repetition of stock phrases and core thematic material that weaves the fabric of both Black American folk sermons and Hopi *tsa'alawu*.

In secular announcements, the prosodic cues (RHF intonational signature, pauses to separate lines not delineated by the RHF, vowel lengthening with each RHF) serve as the primary organizational devices of the announcement. The information ("when it gets light," "go to eat," "don't be shy," "going happily") is presented only once. This is not true of longer public announcements, which are sectioned by words with spatial reference.

In longer Hopi *tsa'alawu*, there is a sectioning device that is based upon the way spatial reference is marked in the language. As noted in chapter 2, only two of the several degrees of spatial distance (proximal and distal) are used in sectioning Hopi narrative discourse. Proximal deictics are used to mark discourse topics at the beginning of each section; subsequent mentions of a topic within the section are marked with distals.

Below is a transcript of a Hopi radio commercial (previously published in Shaul 1988). Proximals (and the nouns they modify) are given as usual in capital letters, and distal expressions are in italic. Each intonational grouping is entered on a single line, and falling intonation is marked with a grave accent ('). Intonational paragraphs are separated by a line space, and marked at the end with a pound sign (#). Each section is numbered with Roman numerals. Some of the proximals (*yangqw*, 'from here,' *yep*, 'here,' *yang*, 'along here') are expected because the speaker, who is broadcasting from Winslow to the Hopi country, considers Winslow to be the locus of not only the broadcast, but also the sponsor.

> Meh, uma Hopisinom:
> Mamant, momoyam, tootim, tàataqt, tsatsayom
> pangqw kiingaqw piw hìisavo inumi tuqayvastotanìiy#

𝄇

> Nu' antsa yangqw umuy sinmuy piw aa'awnani.
I.   Pay IT piw IMA MAATSIWQAT ENGEM — McDonalds —
> me *pam* hapi *pan màatsiwqa* yep Winslow ep
> North Park Plaza epeq
> sinmuy amungem noovalawùu#

𝄇

> Nìiqe oovi yangqw peetuy aw kita,
> Does everybody out there like McDonalds?
> If so, why don't you go into McDonalds for a nice hot
> > breakfast until ten thirty
> > every morning?
> Me uma oovi haqawat
> me pangqw Hopit kiingaqw son inumi qa tuuqayungwa.
> Me uma haqawat pangqw kiingaqw pew sasqaya
> pu' uma haqawat piw yep ökye'
> yep mihikqw tokngwù
> Me' antsa hak pahankive puuwe'
> talavay iits qatupte'
> so'on haqam qa talavay nösniqey wuuwantotangwùu#

𝄇

II   Noq I' YAN MAATSIWQA McDonalds
> North Park Plaza Fourth [Avenue]

naat taawat qa yamakiwtaqw
pay sinmuy amungem hinyungqat hìita noovalawngwùu#

𝟐

III   IMUY TUMALSINMUY amungem
paniqw nu' YANWAT
pu' oovi IT McDonalds ENGEM Hopìituy aawintàay#
Noq oovi uma mee' haqawat Hopìit
paniqw kiingaqw so'on inumi qa tuuqayungwa.
Kur oovi uma haqawat hisat yep yakte'
pu' piw umùutimuy tsamnumye'
YAN taawat naasaptiqw
uma pangsoqw umùutimuy tuutsamyani.
Pay pam pepeq piw tsaatsakmuy amungem hinyungqat hìita
noovatangwùu#

𝟐

IV   Paniqw nu' yangqw YANWAT
pu' oovi antsa umuy Hopìituy
IT YAN MAATSIWQAT ENGEM aawintày,
McDonalds.
Me uma Hopìit navoti'yyungwa
yang pahankimi yaktaqam
me' hak pahankiva waynume'
so'on pahaanat noovayat hìntaqat qa angqw yukut
pu' ahoy piw yangqw pahanakingaqw kiimiq ahoy nimangwù.
Mee' uma haqawat pepeq kiiveq
so'on peetuy sinom pahaanat noovayat hìntaqat qa palkiwyungwa.
Kur oovi uma hisat yakte'
hìita kwangwanönösaniqey wuuwantote'
uma pangsoq put novakit aqw nöswisnìi#
McDonalds pam hapi àasakis pan talöngvaqw
sinmuy amungem hìnyùngqat hìita noovatangwù.
V   Pu' piw IMUY TSAATSAYOM sòosoyam IT SANDWICHES
HINTAQAT ANGQW yukuniqey wuuwantota.
Paniqw nu'yangqw YANWAT
pu' oovi antsa IT MCDONALDS ENGEM
pu' umuy Hopìituy pu' piw aa'awnàay#

You Hopi people
Girls, women, boys, men, children
from up here you will again listen to me for a little.

I   I'm announcing to you people from here again
FOR THIS ONE CALLED McDonalds
that so-called one here in Winslow
at North Park Plaza
makes food for people.

So that's why (I) say,
Does everybody out there like McDonalds?
If so, why don't you go into McDonalds for a nice hot
breakfast until ten thirty
every morning?
Those of you
from up there at Hopi are listening to me.
Those of you who commute from there to here
once you get here,
and spend the night;
whoever sleeps over in town
and gets up in the morning
will surely want something to eat.

II   THIS ONE CALLED MCDONALDS
(at) North Park Plaza, Fourth (Avenue)
before the sun is up
makes all kinds of foods for people.

III   For THESE WORKING PEOPLE
so THIS WAY I
tell you Hopis FOR THIS ONE, McDonalds.

❚

You Hopis
up there are listening to me.
if you ever come (here)
  and if you bring your kids
    THIS WAY at noon
      you will collect your kids.
That one there, for children,
  makes all kinds of food.

❚

IV   So from here I THIS WAY
to you Hopis
announce FOR THIS ONE CALLED
McDonalds.
You Hopis know (that)
those who come to town
if someone comes to town,
  they will want to sample Anglo food
    before going home from here in town.
Some of you up there
surely have a craving for Anglo food.
So if you come down,
  and want something good to eat,
    you will go to eat at this restaurant.

❚

That one McDonalds regularly in the morning that way
makes all kinds of food for people.
V   All THESE KIDS wanna taste all kinds of THESE SANDWICHES.
So from here I, IN THIS WAY have,
FOR THIS ONE CALLED MCDONALDS
announced to you Hopis again.

The information in the commercial consists of several themes: "listen to me," "McDonalds makes food for people," and "kids like Anglo sandwiches." Various renderings of "food" (various kinds of food) and "people" (working people, commuters, people who bring their children to town) are used for variety. The first four deictically defined sections after the introduction (first three lines) use an iteration of "listen to me" followed by a version of "McDonalds makes . . . "; only in the fifth (and last) section does the speaker focus on children, implying that they **like** McDonalds just as Anglo children do. The discourse (global) topic of the piece is, of course, McDonalds; this is the only referent that is consistently introduced with proximal marking and subsequently marked with distals throughout. There are secondary topics ("working people" in III; "children" and "sandwiches" in V) that are introduced with proximals but which have no subsequent mention. There is also a clustering of proximals at the end of the commercial, as can occur in the coda of a traditional Hopi narrative.

The deictically defined sections correlate well with the prosodically defined paragraphs. The introduction is separated from I by an RHF, and both tactics for defining sections coincide in the case of II, III and IV; the diagnostic RHF is one clause away from the beginning of I and two clauses away from the beginning of V. In addition there are section internal RHFs in both I and V. Thus both prosodically and syntactically defined sections in this representative example of a Hopi radio commercial (all adapted only slightly from the traditional *tsa'alawu*) coincide well. One may infer that longer examples of public announcements would have deictically defined sections that correlate with prosodic paragraphs, but that prosodic cues are the genre signatures and the only delineating device used in shorter examples. This inference holds true in three announcements from the previously unpublished Hopi texts of Henry R. Voth (Voth ms.), transcribed below.

The first text is a spring-cleaning announcement from Second Mesa (Voth ms.), here transcribed into Third Mesa dialect. Only one distal marking of subsequent mentions occurs (sixth line of the second part), illustrating the importance of relative length for deictic marking in Hopi discourse.

Pang kur uma naat sinom qa tookya.
Nu' YAN umuy aa'awnani.
Qaavo yaw yep talöngvaqw
uma momoyamu,
mamantu,
iits noovatotaqw
 itam nöönösat
 yukyiq paniqw Torivamiqö.

❡

Yaw itam nööngantani.
YAN itam IMUY as hisat itanamuy nàapiy epehaq kiiyamuy
aqw itam qenitoynayani, yaw'i.

❡

Itam aqw qenitoynaye'
put akw sópkyawat sinom mongwvastotini, yaw'i.

❡

YANHAQAM pu' YEP itanam lavaytaqa'e
itamuy sópkyawatuy sinmuy öqalantota.
Pay YAN'INI!

❡

You people probably have not yet gone to sleep.
I, IN THIS WAY, will announce to you:
Tomorrow HERE when it's dawn
you women,
girls,
early, when (you've) made food,
    and after we have eaten,
        (we will go) to Toriva's spring.

❡

We will be going out.
THIS WAY we will want to clean out the houses of THESE,
our fathers.

❡

If we do the cleaning,
because of it all people will benefit.

❡

Because our fathers have spoken HERE IN THIS WISE,
all of our sundry will be strengthened.
So it will BE LIKE THIS!

The following short oration was performed after the cleaning of the spring had been completed (Voth ms.).

> Ta'a, pay hapi itam YEP itanamuy kiiyamuy aqw ayó' qenitoynaya.
> Oovi tuwat *puma* awyani
> Itamumi nöngakye'
>   YANG itàanatwaniy talahoynayay,
> paalay tuwat YAN hikwnayani.
> Noq put akw *puma* naawungwintani
> su'an naatukwsinayat
>   put [akw] itam naavokyawinkyangw
>   piw pay PEQHAQAMI sópkyawa [noun missing] [verb missing].
> Oovi itam yanhaqam tunatkyàakyangw
>   hàalaykyàakyangw
>   öqaltotini.
> Pay oovi YAN [himu ùutsayom] [verb missing].
> Kwakwhay.

◪

> Okay we really HERE have cleaned out our fathers' houses.
> That's why *they* will go;
> If they come out to us,
>   ALONG HERE they will awaken our prayers to the new day;
> we will drink their juice THIS WAY.
> By means of it they will raise each other up
> and when (they) have grown to just the right maturity,
>   with it we will live life to the fullest.
>   and again TOWARD HERE all [people will benefit].
> So as we pray,
>   as we are happy,
>   we will be strengthened.
> [Reading uncertain].
> Thank you.

The third of the Voth examples is the announcement for a communal hunt (Voth ms.). The first of four sections addresses the announcement to the public. The second sets the plan, and the third covers the actual ground of the hunt journey. The fourth section is a closure.

Yaahahà!
Pangsoq piw inumi tuqayvastota'a!

☒

Nu' yaw umuy aa'awnani:
qaavo yaw itam IMUY SOWIITUY, TAATAPTUY oovi yaktani.
Qaavo yaw talöngvaqw IMA MOMOYAM iits qöötotaqö
noovatotaqö
itam nöönösat
yukyiq taavangqöymiq pönawit nööngantani.
Pangsoq yaw itam yumosa pönawityakyangw
Ma'öpnamurumi yaw itam tsovawmani.
Pangsoq itam tsováaltit
pu' àapiy teevenga póngokt
salàytotini, yaw'i!

☒

Pàapiy yaw itam amùupa hàalaytiwiskyàakyangw
Isvave hak[im] ökit
pu' pangqw kwiningva ahoy hopoqyani.
Pangqw itam yumosa amùupa hàalaytiwiskyangw
Ho'ayami itam tunatyawwisni.
Pangso haqam pew sòosokmuy itam uutaqw
pangqaqw itam sòosoyam hàalaykyaakyangw
piw YANG ITAAKIY AQW tsovawmani, yaw'ì.

☒

Uma hakim pu' YEP tohot himu'yyùngqam,
nu' oovi umumi aa'awna.
YANHAQAM oovi uma tunatyawkyàakyangw
pangqe' tuumoklalwani.
Pay YAN'I.

☒

Hallo!
Again listen to me!

☒

133

I'm going to tell you something:
Tomorrow we're going for THESE JACKRABBITS (and)
COTTONTAILS.
Tomorrow at dawn THESE WOMEN
early (will) make fires
and make food
and then after we eat
we will go out along the west road.
We will follow the road directly along it
and assemble at Snakeweed Ridge.
After assembling
we will circle southwest
and luck will be with us!

○

From there as we (go) happily among them
when someone(s) arrive(s) at Coyote Spring,
from there we'll go along the north back to the east.
From there directly we will go happily among them
to Ho'aya with discretion.
Around there we will shut them all in
and from there we will all be happy
coming back HERE TO OUR HOUSES.

○

Those of you who own THESE MOUNTAIN LION (fetishes)
I'm telling you (this)
BECAUSE OF THIS being prudent
you will have (good) dreams.
It's THIS WAY.

The closing is addressed specifically to those with hunting talismans; by
ending this way, the whole piece (which is a positive prognostication of
a successful hunt) makes success inevitable. Proximal marking accompanies all of the important referents. Occasionally, in longer announcements, there are rementions of a topic with distal marking. In the text of
the post-cleaning announcement, the single remention is "they," referring to "our fathers, whose houses we have cleaned"; these are the cloud

spirits upon which the Hopis depend. In the rabbit hunt announcement, the hunters are not treated as discourse topics (not marked with proximal deictics), but the following are: the object of the hunt (rabbits), the women who make breakfast, and hunting fetishes. There are two rementions of places in the middle of the hunt itinerary. Since the announcer develops a theme of discretion (hunting is not a casual affair), the topicalization of the hunters or remention of the prey may be imprudent.

Internal architecture, as evidenced by versification, depends on relative length. One finds chains of three subordinate clauses (both sections in the spring cleaning announcement have three; the post-cleaning speech has one; the hunting announcement has three), four subordinate clauses (the post-cleaning speech has two; the hunting announcement has one), and even five subordinate clauses (in the post-cleaning announcement). For obvious reasons, long chains of subordination occur only in long announcements. The spring-cleaning announcement (fifteen lines) has triplets, the hunting announcement (twenty-six lines) has couplets, triplets, and quatrains, and the post-cleaning speech (thirty-one lines) has couplets, triplets, quatrains, and even one five-line chain. The longer an announcer makes his *tsa'alawu*, the more apt he is to make use of versification.

There is significant internal rhetoric marked by intonational paragraphing (signaled in the manuscripts by obvious pausals, with or without an exclamation point). In the first part of the spring-cleaning announcement, the first section is an address and outline of preparations, the second is a plan, the third an actualization, and the fourth a result. The second part of the spring-cleaning announcement is a single long paragraph that summarizes the work to be accomplished and the subsequent benefits to people. The post-cleaning speech has three intonational paragraphs: address and plan, assembly point, and admonition to be careful. The hunting announcement follows the journey metaphor of traditional Hopi narratives; the first paragraph is an address, the second a plan, the third the actual hunt journey, and the fourth an appeal to those with hunting fetishes. Intonational paragraphing, even if inferred from flat texts, has an internal rhetoric independent of length.

We may now summarize the structural properties of *tsa'alawu*. Discourse topics, as in Hopi traditional narratives, are marked with proximals, and there is always proximal marking (and even a clustering of proximals) at the end of the discourse. The tendency to use chains of subordinate clauses is a feature of all public announcements, but longer chains (of three to five subordinate clauses) depend on the relative length of the announcement. Intonational paragraphing in the genre is always rhetorical. Such paragraphing does not appear to be dependent on the relative length of an announcement, and only in longer announcements is there an interaction of deictically defined sections and intonational paragraphs. The following are the most consistent genre signatures of *tsa'alawu*: the RHF intonation sequence, pausals, future-intentional use of *yaw*, emphatic *-y*, and the optional introducer *yaahahà*. Given that examples of this genre are relatively short, the information content tends to be minimal, but the affective impact is great as a result of the constant prosodic and frequent morphosyntactic cues that promote communal focus and cultural traditions.

The line is the essential unit of *tsa'alawu*; it is defined by both prosodic means (intonation, pausing) and syntactic means (predicates or their equivalent), just as in the narratives. Proof of the psychological reality of the line in traditional Hopi announcing comes from the following announcement, composed by Emory Sekaquaptewa for the public opening of *The Yellow Ware Road*, an exhibition of Hopi ceramic art that opened in 1990 at the Arizona State Museum. The translation is Dr. Sekaquaptewa's; the lines were written out by him exactly as they are reproduced here. (I have added intonation contours from the live performance.)

> Kur piw peqw tuqayvastota huvamu.\
> Nu' yaw piw umuy aa'awnani:
> Uma yaw yuk it kiihut aw sòosoyam kuyvawisni.\
> Yep yaw i' tsatsqapta, Hopit tuhisa'at màatakiwta,
> oovi uma aw yoriwisni.\
> Pay hàalaykyaakyango.\

> 𝄆

> Please give me your attention here.
> I am informing you now [that]
> you are all to come into this building to look.
> Here, the pottery, a Hopi art, is on display.
> So you may come observe.
> Go in happiness.

Even in this brief announcement (which I personally heard performed), many of the features that characterize *tsa'alawu* are present. The topics "building" and "pottery" (both first mentions only) are marked with proximals; other proximals occur as well (lines 1, 3, 4). The characteristic use of *yaw* is also present, and the RHF is used at the end of intonational periods. Indirection (*huvam,* 'you [pl.],' used only in polite commands) is used, and "go happily" formulaically ends the piece. The fact that the native speaker arranged the written version in lines suggests that the line, as a co-occurring syntactic and prosodic unit, is fundamental to all Hopi discourse; the use of proximals also appears to be a primary feature.

INDIRECTION IN DIRECT ADDRESS AND CONVERSATION
In *tsa'alawu,* direct address ('you') is usually signaled by *huvam,* which is a polite form used in invitation and commands. This principle of indirectness (the substitution of other words for the usual pronouns for 'you': *um, ung; uma, umuy*), distinguishes other Hopi genres of direct address as well. The principle of indirection, usually using indefinites such as "someone" for direct address when there is a known, specific addressee in the actual context of speaking, is a way of removing direct reference to the addressee for purposes of either criticizing or being deferential and polite. The principle is found in *tsa'alawu* and proverbs, though not in private prayers, which are not uttered in public.

The Hopis do not value direct confrontation. They believe that everything is interrelated in a cosmic ecology. Within this system, human beings have volition and may choose between harmonious and inharmonious behavior. Disease and even death or natural calamity may result from an individual not having a "good heart." Directly berating another person may result in misfortune or illness. Once I witnessed a Hopi telling of having accused another person of lying; the accuser then stated "I suppose I'll have a bad Bean Dance," since personal conflict is considered to spoil a ceremony. The Hopis in general avoid direct speech acts when confronting someone else in a situation that has any potential for conflict. This is also evident in the enculturation of Hopi children.

> There are two situations which in their negative importance seem to stand out in the mind of the Hopi, while White children pay comparatively little attention to them. Being disciplined by others and being attacked with "bad" words and jokes causes them much sadness, anger, and pain . . .
> Hopi discipline is exerted to a considerable extent by the group and

137

lies in the imprint of "good" or "bad" which the child obtains in the eyes of the whole community . . . The group judges, advises, teases the individual who has transgressed the common rules or has aroused displeasure . . . judging and teasing are encouraged, if not directly, then indirectly through the practices of the adults and the clowns' festivals. (Thompson and Joseph 1944:103–4)

This philosophy is also evident in common statements made by Hopi speakers:

Pay pi sutsep amùupa sinmuy wùukukikiwnuma.
'(S/he's) always walking all over people.'

𝍖

Pay hakiy aw wùukuke' itsivutingwu.
'(When you) walk all over people, they get angry.'

The lack of an overt grammatical subject in both of these statements avoids any direct reference, so that one must be inferred. Familiarity, however, may make it possible to be more direct with a person.

Pay nu' umuy pas paas naakyaviwaqe oovi'o,
  pay pas umumi naahingqawngwu paapi.
Because I have become familiar with you,
  I have come to be able to criticize you.

The words *pas paas*, 'very, very much/carefully,' underscore the familiarity; the use of the two intensifiers indicates the intimacy of the relation in the sense of English "very, very much."
Indirection is also favored in making a request.

Nu' as uumi hìita tungla'yta, sen um inungem piktani.
I'm just begging a favor of you; maybe you'll make me some piki.

The indirection is the use of *hìita*, 'something.' The first part of the gloss means, literally, "I'm begging something from you." The consultant who gave this example stated: "It's circumlocuted; that's the way we do our asking."

Indirection is used in making invitations as well. In the following example from a traditional narrative, the speaker (Coyote) shifts to indirect address (with *hak*) momentarily, and then shifts back to direct address (with *um*).

Pay **hak** qa sööwunit tuwat kiikinumtongwuy.
Noq um as nuy sukw ùukutay angqw maqani, kwaats.
(Malotki and Lomatuwa'yma 1984:4)

🖉

Don't **you** hesitate to come visit.
By the way, could I have one of your quills, chum?

In the second line, Coyote shifts back to informality (use of the second person pronoun for direct address). This mixing of styles (indirection with familiarity) characterizes the lackadaisical Coyote.

The use of indirection may also function as a marker of politeness. The following is a note written to a colleague:

Hak hàalaykyangw Kyalapongniyat angqe waynumngwu.
Piw hak paasningwu, nen qa haqam unahìntingwu.
Ason um pituqw nu' uumi yorikni.

🖉

You will happily travel in California.
Be careful, and take care of yourself.
I will see you when you get back.

In this short note, the writer shifts to direct address (with *um*) in the last clause, only after the addressee's imagined return.

Traditionally admonitions, like proverbs, are indirectly framed in the third person, even though spontaneous translation into English by a consultant may be imperative in form:

"Hakim qa naatatami'yyungwa," pay pi sutsep umutahay itamuy
aa'awinma.

🖉

"Don't neglect each other," this is what your uncle was
always telling us.

The indefinite address (*hakim*, 'some people,' for *uma*, 'you') was translated as an English imperative spontaneously.

The principle of indirection may be more precisely stated as follows:

Use grammatical markers of indirection.
Detach each clause of a (potentially) confrontational speech act
from its context with irrealis marking.

"Indirect" here means not only diffusing directness by using third person forms, but also maximizing indirection by using indefinite pronouns.
"Irrealis marking" means using modals of uncertainty (*as*, 'conative,' *sen*,
'maybe yes, maybe no,' *kur*, 'probably') or else a negative marker such as
qa, 'not' (*so'on* is the negative marker used with the future tense *-ni*), and
a tendency to use the future (*-ni*) or habitual tense (*-ngwu*). In the example above about going to California, the verbs are in habitual tense
(*-ngwu*), except the last which is in future tense (*-ni*). The subject is *hak*,
'one,' instead of *um*, 'you.' The modals and irrealis marking are omitted,
however, if the speaker has direct (personally observed) evidence for berating a hearer (potential addressee). Additional examples of grammatical
indirection follow.

Hak sunat siivat inungaqw uu'uya.
Someone stole twenty dollars from me.

It is, of course, possible to accuse someone directly of stealing. One consultant stated that the direct forms below "really puts it on the line."

Um pas uuyingwu.
You're quite a thief.

🔊

Um nu'an uuyingwu.
You're nothing but a damn thief.

🔊

. . . taq um kya uu'uyngwu.
'cause you'd probably take it.

The use of *pas*, 'very, quite a' (with reference to something pleasant, such as food or sex), in the first example above softens the directness by creating an ironic effect. In the second example, *nu'an*, 'no count, good-for-nothing,' contributes to a rather startling directness. In the third example, the modal *kya*, 'probably,' provides another case of indirection, in an otherwise direct confrontation.

The deprecation of the addressee can also vary in degree.

Pas kur hak hin hisat hìita ep naamaskyavanangwu.
You are bound to get yourself into some sort of scrape.

In this example, the potential for self-damage is stressed by a series of indefinites (*hak*, 'someone,' for *um*, 'you'; *hin*, 'somehow'; *hisat*, 'at some time or other'; *hìita ep*, 'into something'). This is similar to the ironic effect found in Coyote stories, where the trickster is always up to something.

Pas pi nukurwùutaqa himu hìita hintsakngwu
    nìiqe piw pay yanhaqam yuwsi'yta. (Malotki and
                        Lomatuwa'yma 1985:135)

◼

That no-good one is always up to something,
    and now he [shows up] dressed like this.

◼

Pay pi son pam pituni;
    naapas himu hìita hintsakngwu. (Malotki and
                        Lomatuwa'yma 1985:103)

◼

Well, it looks like he won't return;
    somebody must be up to something.

◼

Pas pi ima hìitu piw pay naap haqam hintsaki.
Himu löwason'isaw ngasta hamana'yta. (Malotki and
Lomatuwa'yma 1985:58)

𝟐

You two whatevers are really something,
Some sex-crazed coyotes with no damn shame at all.

In all of these examples, although direct address is not involved except in the last one, the use of indirection to convey criticism makes the story more flavorful and ironic.

Indirection may also be used to express deference. In the following excerpt, there is a reported confrontation between a customary impersonator of Maasaw (a Hopi deity) and the deity. The situation referred to by the speaker is the deity's closing off a cave as a way of testing the sincerity of the impersonator.

Noq yaw I' hak Orayve X yan maatsiwqa yaw put pàntsakngwuniqw
put yaw wa suus pan himu ùuta.
Noq pu' pay yaw pam itsivutiqe
pu' pangqawu,
  "Pay nu' paapu yàasavo it yantsaki.
  "Nu' as ung pa'angwantaqe
  "noq àasakis hak peqw pakiqw
  "um hakiy yàntsanangwu.
"Noq pay nu' oovi it qe'tini," yan yaw pam itsivuti.

𝟐

This Oraibi man did that impersonation, and
someone shut him in more than once.
So then he got angry
and said,
  "I won't do this anymore,
  "I'm trying to help you,
  "and each time someone comes into here, [and]
  "you do this to them.
"So I'm going to quit this," the man uttered in anger. (Malotki and
Lomatuwa'yma 1987b:132)

The speaker shifts momentarily from the pronoun *nu'*, 'I,' to the indefinite *hak* and *hakiy* near the end of the quote; this makes the directness of the ultimate accusation more polite.

In another example of self-deprecation, a plural addressor is coded with an indefinite pronoun.

"Ya itam hìntiqw qa pay hoytotay?
"Taq pi hakim pay haqami qa iits ökignwuy." (Malotki and
Lomatuwa'yma 1984:44)

⫾

"Why don't we get a head start?
"You know it takes us quite a while to get [somewhere]."

In making the request, the speaker shifts to an indirect form in order to soften the request and be deferential to the addressee.

The use of indirection to indicate politeness may also be preserved in reported speech.

Pu' pay oovi ima peetu inumiq pangqaqwa,
    "Pas pi himu hìita aa'antsaningwu."
(Geertz and Lomatuwa'yma 1987:307)

⫾

And those others say about me [mockingly]
    "He really does things wholeheartedly."

In this example, a speaker reports the seemingly polite description of others of his ceremonial involvement. Presumably intonational cues mark the reported speech as sarcastic.

The use of indirection for politeness is also a feature of Hopi conversational style. Most studies of conversation must deal with turn-taking, overlap, desirability of silence, determining next speaker, pursuing a topic, introducing a new topic, ending, discontinuous adjacency pairs (example: the answer to a question being as many as ten lines away), etc. Moreover, much of adult conversation consists of fragments, not well-formed clauses and sentences. There are lexical means of structuring conversation (subordinating conjunctions; fillers such as *ah-ah, umm, er, y'know*; closures such as *well, okay, so, all right*), in addition to the obvious intonational cues. Moreover, it has been shown that **gaze** (eye contact) and stereotyped gestures are used in conversational management as well. Conversation also varies across and even within cultures. Speakers in New York allow for, even encourage **overlap** (several people speaking at the same time); this would be rude in Iowa. Coming directly to the point is the norm in the western United States, but seems "rude" or "mean" to folks in the Midwest. While there are cultures that require periods of silence in conversation, such breaks would embarrass most Americans, and they would attempt to fill in the silence with "small talk."

It is difficult to define conversation as a genre, and yet it must be dealt with in any theory of language use. One fruitful approach is to look at idealized conversations. For example, the speech of caretakers of children acquiring their first language is usually completely well-formed both in sentential and turn-taking structure. In addition to caretaker speech, sample conversations intended for second language learners are examples of the way conversation is thought of prototypically in a given culture.

Below are two such conversations in Hopi, used in the early 1970s to teach Hopi at the University of Arizona. In less idealized conversations, the grammatical subject may be deleted, and indirection may be less widely used.

In the first, someone is admiring the skill of a Hopi silversmith.

A: Um tumala'yta?
B: Owi, um hak tuwat waynuma.
A: Owi, nu' waynuma, pay nu' tuwat kiikinum waynuma.
B: Haw'o, ta'ay, qatu.'
A: Um tuwat hìita tumala'yta?
B: Pay nu' it yantsaki, it ura siplawu, yan tuwi'yyungwa.
A: Is uni, pas himu nukwangwhìnta. (wùuti)
      Pas hapi himu lomahìnta. (taaqa)
B: Pay pi hakiy tuwi'ytaqw himu lomayukiltingwu.
A: Hep owi, oovi pas um nukwangwyuyku. (wùuti)
      Owi, pas um oovi lomayuyku. (taaqa)
      Nu' payni, pay pi um tsangaw tumala'yta.

∅

A: Are you working?
B: Yes, you who are going around.

A: Yes, I am going around visiting.

B: Is that so; well, have a seat.

A: Are you working at something?

B: Yes, I am doing that which, as you will recall, is called silversmithing.

A: Oh dear, it's really turning out nicely. (woman speaking)
    It sure is well made. (man speaking)

B: Well, when one knows how, it usually comes out well.

A: Yes, that's why you're making it so nicely. (woman speaking)
    Yes, that why you're doing so well. (man speaking)
    Well, I'm going to go; thankfully you are working.

In line 2, the silversmith greets his hypothetical visitor by softening *um*, 'you,' with *hak*. In line 7, the visitor pays a compliment not by saying "you do it well," but by using a passive ("it is done well"), and the smith replies by referring to himself as 'someone' (*hakiy*, line 8; *hakiy* is the emphatic of *hak*).

The second idealized conversation is with a woman engaged in making wafer bread (*piiki*).

A: Is uni, um tuwat pikta? (wùuti)
    Ya um tuwat pikta? (taaqa)

B: Owiya, nu' pikta.

A: Is uni! Pas hapi kwangwawvaqtu. (wùuti)
    Pas hapi kwangwawvaqtuy. (taaqa)
    Sen nu' so'on uumi taytaqw um piktani?

B: As'awu, pay pi so'on hìntini.

A: Is uni, pas hapi um nukwanagwvikta. (wùuti)
    Pas hapi um lomaviktay. (taaqa)

B: Pay pi nu' qa pas tuwi'ykyangw, pay nu hin yukungwu.

A: Oovi pas um nukwangwmupanta. (wùuti)
    Oovi pas um lomamupanta. (taaqa)

B: Hep owi, pay pi tuumat su'an mukitniqw nukwangwmupiltingwu.

A: Pay pi uumi taytaqw sùupan qa hìnta.

B: Yep mùupi, angqw nöösa.'

A: Askwali. (wùuti)
    Kwakwhay. (taaqa)

❡

*:   Oh dear, are you making *piiki*? (woman speaking)
        Are you making *piiki*? (man speaking)
B: Yes, I am making *piiki*.
A: Oh dear! It really smells good. (woman speaking)
        It sure smells good. (man speaking)
        May I watch you while you make *piiki*?
B: Yes, it won't do any harm.
A: Oh dear, you sure make it nicely. (woman speaking)
        You sure make nice *piiki*. (man speaking)
B: Well, I don't really know how, but somehow it comes out well.
A: That's why you're rolling it so nicely. (woman speaking)
        That's why you're rolling it so nicely. (man speaking)
B: Yes, when the stone is just hot enough, then it rolls up nicely.
A: From watching you, it seems easy.
B: Here is a roll, have it to eat.
A: Thank you.

It is the visitor (line 1) who softens *um*, but not with *hak*. Instead, the visitor uses *tuwat* 'in turn'; this adverb conveys a feeling of humility on the part of its utterer. When the visitor pays a compliment with direct address (line 9), the *piiki* maker replies with indirection: "if the stone is just right in heat, then it rolls up nicely." In both well-formed conversations, indirection is used to soften initial contact and to respond to compliments. I can personally remember admiring the work of a kachina doll carver; when I said *Pay hak hìita lomayukungwu* ("Well, someone sure makes it well"), the carver replied that he remembered his grandparents speaking this way. Indirection is valued in traditional Hopi culture as a way of indicating respect and a humble demeanor. It is used in conversation and direct address genres, but the cultural motivation behind the principle of indirection is also found in traditional Hopi narratives.

In traditional Hopi narratives, protagonists are presented in a deferential manner. Self-image is frequently threatened, often through the metaphor of danger to the human body. In a study of the individual in traditional Hopi narrative, Postal (1965), examining the extensive corpus of Hopi traditional narratives in English, found that conscious self-control and discipline were the keys to the survival of protagonists. The action in traditional narrative may be seen as ritualized behavior in which the protagonist's security is threatened. The protagonist's typical response is typically indirect; head-on conflict is not valued. "[A]rguing, it is said, is never justified for it 'warms you up inside.' Patience and a *restraint* of anger are valued . . ." (Postal 1965:459). And, "without a good-heart [knowledge, temperance, courage, awareness], individuals are unable to resist the influence of evil and they will be susceptible to the temptations of misconduct . . . harm to self is seen as having its source in out-going actions or impulses" (1965:456).

The Hopi maximization of indirection as a behavioral norm for dealing with conflict is institutionalized in traditional literature.

As mentioned above, there are three grammatical characteristics of indirection in Hopi: the distancing of a speech act through the use of irrealis tenses (future, habitual), through the use of indefinites (especially to code a direct addressee), and through the use of modal particles to soften the directness of the utterance. It has been proposed that the use of **temporal deixis** (verb tenses) is a universal means of creating politeness in speech acts such as requests (Koike 1989), where politeness is the relation (iconically, distance) between the two interacting parties. For example, Ushie (1986) shows how indefinite expressions are used in naturally occurring English language texts to create a shift or discontinuity that reflects a change in the text producer's point of view or the changed status of a discourse referent. This model would accommodate the Hopi data; indefinite references in Hopi appear largely to create a shift in point of view (such as that due to politeness).

Modals (in the widest sense) are often used in the world's languages to soften direct address. A good example is the French conjunction *mais*, 'but,' used with another particle to indicate agreement at the beginning of an utterance (*mais oui, oui mais, mais d'accord*; Vicher and Sankoff 1989); the tacit agreement facilitates conversational negotiation. In a similar way, English speakers often soften a stressed *but* with a conversational hedge: "I hate to criticize, but . . ." (Lauerbach 1989).

Indeed, indirection as a theoretical issue assumes that meaning lies in active audience/hearer participation. Brenneis (1986) outlines three main types of indirection: text-oriented indirection (such as riddles in Western culture), voice-centered indirection (where the person reference for the utterance is unsure or unclear, such as in the utterance of a spokesperson or in coperformance such as gossip or phatic question-answer pairs), and audience-centered indirection (where indirection is used for purposes of politeness or deprecation; examples include English *now that you mention it, sorry to say, but,* both of which direct criticism at an addressee by softening it with indirection). Yet there must be a cultural component in any universal theory of indirection; Lauerbach notes that no matter what means are used to diffuse directness, the use of indirection involves "possibly culturally determined assumptions pertaining to the individual as a free agent" (1989:42).

In Hopi culture, ideal behavior is focused on nonaggression and the consequent use of language to diffuse interpersonal conflict, owing to what Emory Sekaquaptewa, in the film *Hopi: Songs of the Fourth World,* has called "cooperation without surrender," the collective focus of Hopi culture.

MINIMAL DIRECT ADDRESS GENRES

In addition to *tsa'alawu* and conversation, there are several other direct address genres in Hopi ethnoliterary practice. These include shorter prayers (*unangwvàasi,* 'heartfelt wish, prayer'), proverbs (better termed admonitions), polite formulaic expressions, sayings, and orations. Of these, only orations are usually of any considerable length. Oration and prayer will be discussed below; in this section, we will look briefly at the other minimal direct address genres. Virtually the only deictics used are proximal, thus substantiating the theory that proximals mark first mention of discourse topics, even if there are no subsequent distal rementions. The principle of indirection is especially noticeable in private prayer, where it is suspended. A speaker is free to use direct address (*um,* 'you') since there is no public around to overhear.

The genre marker of private prayers is the word *ta'a,* 'okay,' which is found in the opening line. Because the word connotes familiarity, it is probably not appropriate for a public context.

The following is a prayer that is usually offered unspoken before eating (Voth ms.).

Ta'a pas pay han it toko'ykyangw
    soona'ykyangw
        sutsep yephaqam hàalayni.
Pu' IMA NANA'IVOQ OO'OMAWTU
itamuy ookwatutwe'
    YANG yoknayaqw'ö.

📓

Pu' YEP IMA YANG TUTSKWAT SOOSOVIQ ANG hìitu
poninitotaqamu
tuwat qatsiy, naavokyawwintotani.

▯

Okay, having THIS as meat
having THIS as sustenance,
(I) will always be happy.
IF THESE CLOUDS FROM ALL AROUND
pity us,
it will rain ALONG HERE.

▯

THESE ONES LIVING ALL OVER ALONG THIS LAND
here residing
will enjoy the benefits of life.

▯

In this prayer, there are two intonational paragraphs with some subordination. The tenor is general, and there is no definite addressee. As in public announcements, there is a call for attention, a message, and then a generic closure.

Other prayers have definite addressees. Burying children occasions conventional prayers (Voth ms.).

Ta'a, um YEP itamuy maatavi.
Oovi um ngas'ew hìisavo YEP na'uytani.
Piw ason um ahoy itamumini.
Um ahoy itamuminiqw
itam ephaqam sòosoyam yestapnumyani.
Pay nu' ung kyàakyawna.

▯

Okay, you have discarded us HERE.
That's why at least you will hide yourself HERE
[for a while].
And after a while you will come back to us.
When you come back to us,

we will go around settling from place to place.
I miss you.

The use of proximals implies that life is most comfortable at one's home base; life outside one's village is called *maqasqatsi* 'life of fear' (recall the journey metaphor of Hopi narration). This feeling is the primary tone of prayers as heartfelt, personal discourse.

A subtle difference is found in a prayer for children who have been initiated but who have not reached adult status (Voth ms.).

Ta'ay.
Hinoqw um itamuy YEP öönati?
Oovi um yàapiy sutsvo qatsit awhaqami nawusni, awhaqamnit'a

𝟕

angqw itamuy IT QAA'ÖT, KWAWYVATNGAT,
MELOONIT AKW itamuy ookwatwni.

𝟕

Okay.
Why did you tire of us HERE?
So from here on out you will be resigned to life, to wherever,

𝟕

from this place, pity us with THIS CORN,
WATERMELONS AND MELONS.

𝟕

This prayer acknowledges that life goes on, a convention that is familiar to the speaker; the structure is shorter and informal (in terms of the factors so far treated). Note that there are two intonational paragraphs; the break between "to wherever" and "from there" follows from the internal rhetoric, representing the distance between the afterlife and the speaker's present situation.

Similarly brief are prayers to the generalized dead at various major ceremonies. According to Voth, the following prayer would be appropriate at the Soyal or Flute Ceremonies (Voth ms.). The petition is specific; the continuity with present life is stated.

Ta'a nu' IT umugem yuku.
Uma IT AKW ahoy itamuy
IT QAA'ÖT, KAWAYVATNAGAT, MELOONIT,
SIPAALAT AKW itamuy PEW ookwatutwani.

🮲

Okay, I have made THIS for you.
You, by means of this, will
with THIS CORN, WATERMELONS, MELONS,
PEACHES pity us HERE.

This short direct admonition is obviously impersonal. It is addressed to a general audience. Why then the use of *uma*, 'you,' a direct form? Because of the presumption of personal contact with the addressee. The speaker does not know the addressee; how does one account for such a presumption? Here the implicit assumption is that privacy implies directness. The direct form (*uma*, 'you'), not the indirect form (*hakim*, 'some people'), is used because there is no public present.

Prayers offered to the kachinas are obviously both personal and public. The following is a prayer to the Badger Kachinas, who are the foremost of physicians (Voth ms.).

Pay hapi uma tuwat IT NGAHUT tuwi'yyungwa.
Oovi IMA YEP ITAATIM *put akw* paapu qa tuutuyyani.
Oovi uma YANHAQAM tunatyawkyangw
    angqe' yaktani.

🮲

You really know THIS MEDICINE.
So *by means of it* THESE OUR CHILDREN HERE will not
                get sick.
That's because you will be looking out (for them) as
    you go about.

The two discourse topics ("medicine" and "our children") are both marked amply with proximals. Only one is rementioned, coded as a distal, showing that even in minimal discourse the more general principle of topic marking is germane.

The following prayer to the Red Fox Kachina is for success in hunting that species (Voth ms.).

Hak ha'e!
Pay hapi okiw nu' IMUY YANG SISIKYAATATUY sutsep amungk
              YANNUMA.
Oovi pas pay okiw nu' ùupe salàytini.

⁊

Hark!
Verily I am humbly always GOING AROUND HERE after THESE
              RED FOXES AROUND HERE.
So I humbly will be fortunate in my luck with you.

In this prayer, the utterer is humble (*nu'*, 'I,' co-occurs with *okiw*, 'poor'). The use of proximals is the other predominant feature; topic saliency correlates with the urgency or earnestness of the message.

To summarize, prayers are usually single intonation paragraphs. Discourse topics are always marked with proximals, frequently several. This may signal psychological saliency (prayers are in earnest) as well as discourse saliency. The principle of coding rementions in a single section with distals is still valid, despite the brevity of the genre. Where intonational paragraphing occurs (as indicated by major pausal constructions), there is a rhetorical motivation. Prayers often begin with the genre signature *ta'a* 'all right' or the equivalent *hak na'e*.

Public prayers are longer. The genre signature *ta'a* is used, and all of the important mentions are marked with proximals; there are no rementions with distals. Long public prayers use versification into quatrains or multiples of four for great rhetorical effect, and are, in this sense, the sectioning device in public prayers. Content tends to be limited to culturally desired themes. The formulaic ending "go (along) happily" is also a genre signature of the public prayer. The reader is referred to the example of a public prayer in chapter 3.

Hopi proverbs have indirect reference for entities directly addressed in a public context as a genre signature, through the use of indefinite pronouns (*hak*, 'someone'; its plural is *hakim*; the singular objective form is *hakiy*, which must be carefully distinguished from the emphatic form *hak'i(y)*; the plural objective form is *hakimuy*), because logically, the referent is genuinely indefinite. The Hopi term for this genre is *maqastu-tavo* 'admonition.'

> Aw qa kwangwataytaqa pay pas put son hinwat qa sasvini.
> "Someone with a bad outlook usually manages to knock something."

𝟏

> Hak Kayaamuyva mihikqw qa ngumantangwu, ispi hak yaw
> paasatniqw Maasawuy amum
> ngumantangwu.
> A woman should not grind corn at night during the month
> of Kyaamuya, because they say
> that she would be grinding
> with Maasaw. (Malotki and
> Lomatuwa'yma 1987b:90)

In these two examples (there are more in Malotki and Lomatuwa'yma 1987b:88–92), the subject of both clauses is indefinite. Yet when applied in context, the referent could be definite, with the indefinite pronoun coding direct address (*hak* or *hakim* instead of *um*, 'you,' or *uma*, 'you [pl.]'). There is another characteristic feature of proverbs: there is always a statement of prohibition and then a statement of consequences.

The importance of indirection is also seen in polite formulaic expressions, addressed to a person in context.

> Ta'ay, angqw neengem oya'a.
> Help yourself (to food).

𝟏

> Itamuy a'ni öqala.
> Good wishes.

𝟏

> Hak öqawmangwu!
> Go in strength!

In the first example, direct address is avoided by using *neengem*, 'for one's self,' which occurs with a command (*oya'a*, 'place it,' *oya*, 'to place'), which would normally involve the use of *um*. In the second example, the objective form of *itam*, 'we' (*itamuy*), is used in an unusual way: the objective form functions as an **inclusive** usage ('you and I' = 'we'), as opposed to **exclusive** usage ('s/he and I' = 'we, not you'). In the last example, we find one of the common means of indirection (indefinite pronouns). In all three examples, the problem of softening direct address is present, while the solutions are various. In the first two cases, more idiomatic tactics are followed, while in the third the conventional, fully productive means of indirection is used.

The minimal address genres are prayers, proverbs, and sayings. Prayers are distinguished in that they may begin with *ta'a*, consist of several usually compound and/or complex sentences, and with topics marked by proximals that are not rementioned. Proverbs and polite **formulaic expressions** are always a single sentence in length and always use indirection for politeness; proverbs, as admonitions, are always negative in form. Prayers, however, do not often use indirection because, even though they may be made in public, they are not audible enough to be heard.

Sayings are formulaic expressions similar in length to proverbs and polite expressions. A saying is a single, conventional statement tending not to be completely opaque referentially (as is the case with total idiomaticity). They are an emotive response expressing a cultural value.

Tooki momost naamaspaya.
"Last night the cats threw themselves over the cliff."

Ø

Tsangaw pi hak put qa nötsvu.
"Thankfully no one aborted her/him."

Ø

Tuunösvongya tuuqayvani.
"The food will start talking."

Ø

Pay um inungem tsangaw mongvastini.
"May you benefit from me."

In the first of these, coined by a person known for humor, a foreign accent (Anglo, Black, or Mexican) is used; the humor lies in someone with a "foreign" accent trying to pronounce Hopi. The second is uttered when someone does a favor for the speaker; had the person been aborted, they would never have been able to perform the favor. The third is a statement about food left on the table uneaten; it will start to take part in the conversation. The fourth is a traditional utterance that advises turning the other cheek as a response to aggression; it is said out of the culprit's hearing.

ORATION AND PUBLIC PRAYER

An example of Hopi oration is given in chapter six. The information structure (thematic structure as defined by proximals and distals) is exactly like that of traditional Hopi narratives and the longer *tsa'alawu*: discourse topics are introduced within a section by or as proximals, and remention within a section is marked with distals. There are eight sections. The version given in the schematic below is a paraphrase of the English translation.

I   THESE WHO WORK AT ANGLO JOBS (and others)
     benefit from the English language . . .
II   When one ponders THIS (the use of Hopi
     in contemporary Hopi life) . . .
III ALL THESE IDEAS of adapting Hopi
     creatively for current needs
       (written Hopi, taped Hopi, neologisms) . . .
IV   THIS LANGUAGE of songs is also creative . . .
V   THE LANGUAGE of joking is creative . . .
VI   THESE WAYS OF TRADITIONAL KNOWLEDGE and
     THIS THING CALLED LIFE as we know it depend on
     the Hopi language . . .
VII THIS LANGUAGE, if forgotten, will mean
     in the future the Hopis will have no
     identity . . .
VIII THESE WHO ARE YOUNG can at least learn
     some Hopi in the home . . .

All of these sections are clearly defined by interaction of topic and proximal marking; the section topic is always rementioned at least once with a distal expression. There is one clustering of proximals at the end of a section for an emphatic summary (section III), and frequently *yan* or *yan-haqam*, 'in this way,' is used to highlight the situation described by the speaker. Just as often, *pan(haqam)*, 'in that way,' is used as a distal repetition of the situation discussed in the section. Both *yan(haqam)* and *pan(haqam)* function in these cases as adverbial proforms.

Intonational units (shown in the transcription as single lines ending in a comma, period, colon, semicolon, or exclamation mark) correlate almost entirely with the syntactic lines. In two instances, however, an intonational contour resembles the rise-hold-fall genre signature of *tsa'alawu*, and in a third case, there is a juxtaposition of two clauses with different subjects without the usual verb marking for this situation. Both of these occur very early in the oration. The first instance is given below.

> Sampi Pahaant qatsi'at, tuhisa'at tuyqawvaq'ö.
> Itam sòosoyam pu' Pahaanat aw tuutuqayya.
>
> 𝌆
>
> It is so because the whiteman's lifestyle and inventions have
>   prevailed everywhere.
> All of us today are learning about the whiteman.

Notice that the break, indicating an intonational break, syntactically correlates with a pausal form. Rhetorically, the first clause before the break is the condition that occasions the state of affairs in the second clause. In the second intonational-syntactic break (marked by an exclamation point), the rhetorical force of the break is that the succeeding part summarizes and reinforces the first part by way of giving a consequence.

> Itam put peenaye'
>   pu' put tutuvenlalwakyangw
>   itàakiikiy ang put pongya'yyungwni!
> Akw itam itàatimuy pentutuwnayakyangw
>   pu' piw tungwantutuwnayani.
>
> 𝌆
>
> If we put it to writing,
>   then as we produce it in written form,

we can keep it on display in our homes!
With it, we can teach our children to write
and to read.

Here major intonational breaks correlate rhetorically with a syntactic feature (the pausal in the first example); there is no syntactic and intonational mismatch or overlap of the units delineated by either system; the intonational contours follow the syntactically defined units.

A third seeming syntactic-intonational mismatch occurs toward the very end of the piece, in the seventh (deictic) section. It is used rhetorically to indicate the overwhelming quality of the Anglo culture invading Hopi.

Sòosoy tuwi'am lavayit ep akw sinom naatuwi'ywisqat, pam ang tuuvoyni.

🛈

Without people recognizing their people with language, he will vanish.

Everyone's kin (and ken) is grounded in their language, (and without it) the Hopi will vanish. This is an example of juxtaposing two clauses with different subjects without the different subject marker -qw. "One will vanish" is set off as a separate intonational unit. (A more literal translation of this is: "(without) the people's situation in the world of their entire knowledge, it/she/he would vanish.")

In these three examples, the rhetorical effect is both summarizing and emotional. In the first case, the mismatch functions as an abstract for the whole talk. In the second example, the mismatch reinforces the consequence of the preceding clause, which is the theme of the talk. In the last example (very near the end of a fairly lengthy text), the mismatch functions as a warning and admonition not to lose the language; it draws attention to the content. In both the second and third example, the information conveyed, although prominent in terms of information management, is also highly charged with emotional meaning, as is obvious from the translation. As in the case of narratives, these "mismatches" have a major rhetorical impact on the (con)text in which they occur.

In terms of subordination, there are many quatrains in the structure of the piece. There are two main patterns. One is for a quatrain to modify a single clause/line preceding it. The following example is from the middle of section II; it is presented in English translation.

Qa *panwat* YANIKT
pu' sen itam IT HAKIY TÖNAYIT KWUSUNGWUQAT akw
yu'a'atotaqw
pam itamungem lavayit tangalawqw
pu' hak hìita navotninikt.

▮

If that will not be THE WAY,
then we might speak into THIS WHICH CAPTURES THE VOICE
so that it will accumulate the language for us,
and when someone wants to know something, (one can listen).

In this example, the quatrain of successive subordinate lines forms a potential consequence of the first clause of the example.

In the second quatrain pattern, the successive subordinate clauses function rhetorically as a single unit; the pattern may also be used in parallel. The two examples below are from section III; the first is in the middle of the section, and the second example is at the very end.

Hìita puuhut alöngöt aw ökye'
pu' aw tuvotye'
pu' hin tungwayaqw
put akw pàapiy himu maatsiwngwu.
When they encountered something new and different,
when they had comprehended it,
they would identify it by a name
so that from then on it was called by that.

▮

Puma lavayiy qa peevewnayakyàakyangw
akw qatsiy piptani'ywisqe
haqam himu puhulavayit akwniniqw
qa nanaatsopyat engem yukuyangwu.
They did not lack confidence in their own language
as they characterized their world by it
and when something called for a new name,
they made up one for it without wavering.

The first quatrain in this pair states the theme of the section (using the Hopi language creatively for new things); the other member of the pair, which occurs at some distance from it, echoes the first. The prevalence of quatrains (there are also couplets and triplets), the fact that there are eight deictically defined sections, and the fact that the most significant number in Hopi culture is four and multiples of four all suggest that versification of lines into groupings smaller than sections in Hopi oration, as in Hopi traditional narrative, is often in fourfold units. Again we are reminded that in Hopi tradition versification is a matter of culturewide convention, than a matter of individual style, as Dell Hymes (1981) infers.

The only discrete genre signature used in oration is *me* (*meh*, *me'*), 'hark,' which is translated in the piece as "as you can see" and "listen"; the only other feature is the nearly complete correlation of intonational lines with syntactic lines. This oration was not delivered in the traditional way (from a high point in a village, but as a speech; hence the genre signature is more significant in this example. The use of indirection (indefinite pronouns for possible direct referents such as "you") is clear in this example, but the direct pronouns for 'you' (*um*, *uma*) do occur in other published orations (Lewis 1984, Leslie 1984, Lomaquahu 1985, Lomayaktewa 1985, Sidney 1985). In these orations, sections defined by proximals and distals, as well as versification into quatrains and multiples of four, are nevertheless evident.

The affinity of direct address genres to Hopi traditional narratives is clear, but there are also important differences. Narration suspends the indirection that normally might prevail between the parties of a speech event. Indeed the required interaction of a Hopi narrated event (as a special kind of speech event) consists of feedback from the audience, mainly using a single word (*owi*, 'yes') that is direct in its semantic force. Indirection, the genre signature of public announcements, public prayers, and orations is downplayed in narration, even though normal interpersonal conversation is ideally indirect as well. Narratives are "open" texts, in that they require that a ritualized interaction take place. Direct address genres in Hopi culture, on the other hand, are "closed" in the sense that they facilitate no interaction at all; but they are "open" in that they always are directed toward some addressee(s). Both direct address genres and traditional narratives share major structural features: sectioning by deictics, introduction of discourse topics marked by proximals, line demarcation by the same syntactic and prosodic means, rhetorical significance of the disjunction of these cues, and some identical aspects of subsectional architecture (quatrains defined by subordination and perhaps other features as well).

Yet the audience responds to certain marked points in a fully performed narrative (ends of sections, after quatrains highlighted by a shift to high register, at syntactic-prosodic disjunctions), while they do not respond to the same structural cues in direct address genres. This suggests that Hopis group direct address genres together in an unnamed supergenre distinct from traditional narration. Idealized Hopi conversation, in which indirection (the genre signature for direct address forms) is also indispensable, is thus linked with direct address forms. Yet conversation is distinguished from them because in conversing people must answer each other, whereas in direct address forms the addressee(s) typically remain silent. Much remains to be done in studying audience feedback/response in the delivery of traditional Hopi oration. Much remains to be done in studying audience feedback/response in the delivery of traditional and improvised Hopi oration. Public speaking in Hopi culture, like storytelling, is more ritualized; hence, Hopi conversational style and conversational conventions constitute a separate genre.

6

EMORY SEKAQUAPTEWA'S ORATION

THE FOLLOWING IS THE transcription of an address made by Emory
Sekaquaptewa for the fourth Hopi Mental Health Conference (E.
Sekaquaptewa 1985). It has been transcribed into line format, with subordination indentations; the transcription has been checked with a tape of
the same speech in order to identify intonational units; pauses are indicated
by commas, periods, colons, and semicolons according to their length. There
are several appositives and one listing; appositives and items in lists are intonationally separate lines. The RHF contour is marked by a line space.

Discourse topics distinguished by proximals appear in capital letters;
rementions within a section are in italics. The resulting discourse sections are indicated with a Roman numeral and separated by line spaces.
There are eight resulting sections with an introduction, all of which display rhetorical consistency. The translation is Sekaquaptewa's; some
respelling (umlauts, falling tones) has been inserted.

> Ya sen Hopisinom hinwat pu' YEP aw alöngtote'
> naap lavayiy akw paapu sòosok hìita hintsakpiy ep
> naamongvasnayani?
> Pas hapi qa hak Hopi pu' qa nuutum Pahaanat himuyat hìita
> enang qatu.
> Sòosoyam Hopisinom pahanlavayit naaqavo akw enang
> mongvasya.

I

I   5   Tis IMA PAHANTUMALAT epyaqam.
Pu' pahankiva hìita nöösiwqat pu' himu'ytiwqat oovi
hepnumyaqam.
Sampi Pahaanat qatsi'at, tuhisa'at tuyqawvaq'ö.

🪶

Itam sòosoyam pu' Pahaanat aw tuutuqayya.
Itam hìita himuyat songyawnen aw tungla'yyungwa.
10   Noqw pay suyan itam IT as kya qa YAN naaviptsantotakyàakyangw
pay naat Hopìit qatsiyat aw hin màatsi'ywisqey pay akw enang
nayesni'ywisa.

🪶

II   Pay IT aw wuuwantaniqw
hiihìimu niiltiwta.
Me, hinwat itamye'
15   itàahopilavayiy qa suutokyani?
Sen itam Hopilavayit peenayani?
Itam put peenaye'
pu' *put* tutuvenlalwakyangw
itàakikiy ang *put* pongya'yyungwni!
20   Akw itam itàatimuy pentutuwnayakyangw
pu' piw tungwantutuwnayani.
Qa *panwat* YANikt
pu' sen itam IT HAKIY TÖNAYT KWUSUNGWUQAT akw
yu'a'atotaqw
pam itamungem lavayit tangalawqw
25   pu' hak hìita navotninikt
put akw tuuqaytamantani.
Pu' pay kur piw qa *pantaniqw*
pu' itam sopkyawat Hopisinom Hopilavayit momiq taviyaniqey
aw sunte'
pu' item pas *put* enang tunayyawkyàakyangw
30   talöngwintotani.
Panwat tunatyamiqw
pu' hak pas kur hinqe
àasakis taalat ep Hopilavayit akw enang qatsiy

tumaltaniqey naami
yuki'ykyangw
hìita hintsakmantani.

𝟚

III 35   Pu' hikis pay sòosok YAAYAN AW WUWNIT akw itam
                itàalavayiy ep mongvasyaqw
        pu' sen *pam* haqàapiy öqawi'ymani.
        Panmakyangw
        pu' hikis kya Hopilavayit aw peehu lavayi hoyokiwmani.
        Pay pi son yuupahaqaqw itàawuwu'yam qa hinwat yeewatiwisqw
    40 oovi Hopit lavayi'at sòosok qatsiyat aw angqaqw aptsiwma.
        Hìita puuhut alöngöt aw ökye'
            pu' aw tuvotye'
            pu' hin tungwayaqw
            pu' *put* akw pàapiy himu màatsiwngwu.
    45 Oovi himu sivanamiqlölö:
        siiva naanamiq ngölöykyàakyangw
            aqw namiwiwyùngqe
            put hongvi'yta.
        Pu' himu piw polimsa:
    50 itàakikiy ang sòosoviq u'utspi *put akwsa* hötsiwat aw
                                    wiwkyàakyangw
            akw haayiwyungwa.
        Pu' tis sòosoyam sinom hìita tutuvenkohot akw enang mongvasya.
        Sòosoyam tungwniy pentotakyangw
        akw enang mongvasya.
    55 Pay pi YAAYAN angqaqw Hopisinom sonqe hintsakwisa lavayiy
                                    ep'e
        noqw YANWAT tuhisayamuy aw piptsaniqw
            pay a'ni yeeyewatu.
        Puma lavayiy qa peevewnayakyàakyangw
            akw qatsiy piptsani'ywisqe
    60   haqam himu puhulavayit akwniniqw
            qa nanaatsopyat engem yukuyangwu.

𝟚

163

IV   Pu' antsa I' LAVAYI,
         taatawit epnìiqa,
         pam sumataq pay naat a'ni ö'qala.
65   Hak *panwat* yeeyewatuy amumi kyaataytangwu.
         Himuwa taawi hinwat lavay'oyiwkyangw
           antsa kwangwatöqtingwu;
         hakiy unangwayat su'an tavingwu.
         Pu' himuwa piw lavayit hinwat namikwapte'
70   akw hìita pitsangwayat songyawnen pas pu' piw sonwaqw
           akw lelwingwu.
         Haqawat *put* piw tuwi'yyungwa,
         hin lavayit tutkilalwakyàakyangw
           naanami pitamintota.

                     ❡

V   Pu' I' PIW LAVAYI,
75   akw itam naahàalaynayaqa,
         kunatapi.
         Put ep piw haqawat tutuhistnìiqe
           akw itamuy tiitaptota.
         Hakim *panwat* hìita aw tsuyte'
         pay akw piw mongvastotingwu.
80   Pas qa himu opit qatsiyat ep qa lavayit akw enang
                        pitsangwa'yta.
         Me, itam ang yoyrikyani.
         Ang himu màamatsiwya:
           tutskwa,
             hintsakpi,
85   poninitiwqa,
             a'aniwqa,
             yuykiwqa,
             yeesiwqa,
               sòosoy paavam
90   himu Hopìituy qatsiyamuy ep naap
                          qeni'yyungwa.
         Sòosoy *pam* ayawa'yyungwa.

                     ❡

VI   Noqw yepehaq hapi Hopisinom kur naat hingsakw akw
                     YAAYANTAQAT NAVOTIT
                     ngu'yyungwa.
       Pam himu a'ni nga'ytaqe
       oovi naat hinwat itamungem piw angqw tsiyakni.
95   Niikyangw kya *pam Hopit lavayiyat* ang tunatyat
                     pitsangwa'ykyangw
     angqwte'
       pu' hapi pay naat Hopìituy amumi màatsiwtani.
       Hopit qatsiyat aw songyawnen naaqavo alöng'iwma.
       Sampi I' HIMU QATSINIIQA pay angqaqw *panwat* hoyta.
100   Angqaqw naanangk qatsivaptsiwyungqam nanaapvewat hin
                     tuwat qatsiy ep aw
                     nanaptangwu.
       Pay naat *pan hiniwma.*
       Pu naat yuumoqhaqami piw pay *paniwmani.*

                   ▯

VII   I' LAVAYNIIQA,
       pam kya Hopit naapvewat makiwa'at níiqe
105   hin Hopi qatsi'ymaqw
       pan qatsiyat engem maatakni'yma.
       Kur haqàapiy Hopilavayiy paapu qa aw mongvasnen
       haqami *put* tatamtat
       sùutokye'
110   pàapiy *pam* kur himu'u.
       Kurhin *pam* paapu Hopinìiqey
       panwat maatakiwtani.
       Kur hìita akw sinomuy naami ngu'ytani.
       Sòosoy tuwi'am lavayit ep akw sinom naatuwa'ywisqat,
115   *pam* ang tuuvoyni.
       Qa haqam himu tunsini.
        Kurhin sinom naanangqwvimni.
       Ngyamuy angqw taahamatniqam pu' namatniqam ang
                     sulawtotini.
       Noqw pay tsangaw Hopìit naat hiihìita Hopihintsakpiy aw
                     unangwtavi'yyungqe
120   pay puuvut ang Hopilavayit aw a'ni tatqa'nagwya.

Pu' pay naamahin qa Hopit hintsakpiyat ang enang
     Hopilavayit akw tumalay aw
     antsani'ywisqw
 so'on as hìntani.
Hak Hopihimut angqw alöngöt ep hìita aw Hopivewat wuuwante'
 pay piw put pas hinwat piptsangwu.

125 Paypi Hopi hisat kur hin qatùuqe
 tuwat wa neengem hin wuuwanta.
Kur hin *pam* qa hìita aqw taymakyangw
 yanqe' qalawma.
Noqw oovi put tuwi'ytaqa,

130 aw màatsi'ytaqa naamahin yep pu' hihin alöngöt qatsit
     yesqat ang hinmakyangw
 haqami Hopit engem tunatyaniqw
 pay pam kurhin naat qa pangsoq mamavisni.

🔲

VIII Pay IMA HIHIN TSAATSAYOM,
 YANG PU' ITAMUMI WUNGWIWTAQAM,

135 angsakis kiikiy ang Hopilavayit aw tuutuqayye'
 pay son hìisa'haqam Hopilavayiyat qa ömàatotani.
 Pay *panwat* pi as supsiwta.
Hak yumuy pu' namuy amungaqw lavayit tuuqayvangwu.
Pumuy hak amutsviy qatsiy navotngwu nìiqe

140 oovi wuuyoq'iwmakyangw
 hìita tuwi'yve'
 hak pumuy amumi ahoy put ep tsuyakngwu.

🔲

How might the Hopi people alter their present lifestyle,
 by the use of their own language in everything they do?
 The fact is, there is no Hopi today who is excluded from
     a lifestyle that makes use of
     some things of the Whiteman.
 All the Hopi people benefit by the use of English day
     after day.

🔲

I 5 Especially THESE OCCUPIED IN THE WHITEMAN'S
MANNER OF WORK.
And (THESE) who shop for food and material things in the
whiteman's cities.
It is so because the whiteman's lifestyle, his inventions
have prevailed everywhere.

⌷

All of us today are learning about the whiteman.
We are soliciting, as it were, some things of his.
10 While we surely must see ourselves IN THIS WAY,
yet we also continue to maintain our life according to
the way in which we still
understand the Hopi way of
life.

⌷

II When one ponders THIS,
many things are amplified.
As you can see, how should we go
15 so that we will not forget our Hopi language?
Should we perhaps put the Hopi language to writing?
If we put *it* to writing,
then as we produce *it* in written form,
we can keep *it* on display in our homes!

⌷

20 With it, we can teach our children to write
and also to read.
If *that* will not be THE WAY,
then we might speak into that which captures the voice,
so that it will accumulate the language for us,
25 and whenever someone wants to know something,
s/he can listen *to it.*
Now if *that does not seem the way* [it is]
then if all Hopis agreed to prioritize the Hopi language,
and include *that* in our conscious purpose
30 from day to day.

When *that is the purpose,*
then one must resolve
to include the Hopi in one's daily life and work,
    somehow.

𝄇

III   35   Or even more so, we can make use OF ALL THESE IDEAS
                       with our language,
       so that in time it will gradually become more viable.
As *it does so,*
       other words might even be added to the Hopi language.
In the distant past our ancestors had some creativeness
40   because the language has kept pace with the entire Hopi universe.
When they encountered something new and different,
       and when they comprehended it,
           they would identify *it* by a name
              so that from then on *it* was called by it.
45   That's why there is metal and linked together:
metal that is bent into each other
       by which it is secured
           for strength.
Then there is a thing like butterfly wings [hinges]:
50   in all our homes doors are fastened to doorways
           hanging *by means of them.*
Today, all people have use of the writing stick [pencil] also.
Everyone, when they sign their name,
       benefits.
55   So the ancient Hopis likely did LIKE THIS with their language,
and when one considers their innovations IN THIS WAY
       they were very creative.
They did not lack confidence in their language
       as they characterized their world by it,
60   and when something called for a new word,
       they made one up for it without wavering.

𝄇

IV   And verily THIS LANGUAGE,
       that is in the songs,

it seems to be still going strong.
65 One looks in awe at those who are creative *in that way*.
Sometimes a song sounds beautiful
by the way words are placed together;
it puts one's heart in the right place.
And another will stack words together in a way
70   as if to paint with new beauty some essence.
Some people possess *that skill*
of putting words together
after they first analyze them.

🛡

V   Then also THIS LANGUAGE,
75 the one by which we entertain ourselves,
     jesting.
At it, some are so skillful
     that they pacify us with it.
When people chuckle *in that way*,
     they benefit by it also.
80 There is nothing in the Hopi life that does not have
                              essence by means of language.
Listen, let's look around.
Things have names all around:
     land,
          activity,
85   things in motion,
               things that grow,
                    things that are made,
                         things that are living,
                              all other things
90 that have a place in the Hopi world.
all (those) have a purpose.

🛡

VI   But even now, it is apparent that the Hopi people are
                         still clinging, however
                         little, TO THESE WAYS OF
                         TRADITIONAL KNOWLEDGE

because *it* is a deep-rooted thing,
 it will sprout for us again in yet other ways.
95 But if *it* is to come back,
 it should perhaps have the essential ideal of the language,
 so that it is still named in Hopi.
 Hopi life changes every day.
 But then THIS THING CALLED LIFE has always moved *that*
 way.
100 From the earliest times each following generation has
 experienced their own world in
 their own way.
 It is still *that way* today.
 And it will continue to *be that way* into the future.

𝟐

VII THIS LANGUAGE,
 since it is the Hopi's natural gift,
105 reveals their world
 according *to the way* in which Hopis are conducting
 their life.
 If eventually, a Hopi should no longer have use for his
 or her language,
 then neglects *it*
 and forgets *it*,
110 thereafter s/he is a nonentity.
 It will no longer be possible for *that one*
 to be seen as a Hopi.
 There will be nothing by which to hold his or her
 people to him or herself.
 All of their ways by language through which people
 identify with each other,
115 (that) will (all) disappear.
 Those that are to be one's clanswomen will be nowhere.
 It will not be possible for people to be bound together in clanship.
 Maternal uncles and fathers by clan will become no more.
 But it is gratifying to know that because Hopis are still
 supporting their own Hopi
 activities,

120   they have to depend on the Hopi language in those things,
       even if they use Hopi in nontraditional ways,
       will not matter.
       When one ponders in a Hopi way something that is alien to Hopi
         one can really perceive it differently.
125   Since the Hopi have lived for a long time,
         they must, in their own way, reflect on how it is for them.
       Surely, *they* must have looked to something
         in order to reach where they are today.
       Thus, the one who is familiar with that,
130   even if he lives a different life of today,
         he can still aim his life's goals
           toward that which has been destined for Hopi.

◪

VIII   THESE WHO ARE YOUNGER,
        ONES WHO ARE OUR NEW-GROWN,
135   if *they* would at least regularly hear the Hopi
                               language in their homes,
        they will pick up some amount of the Hopi language.
        It is the easiest way.
        One usually learns from one's mother and father.
        One realizes one's life because of them
140   so that as one grows older
            and learns things,
              it is to them that one is grateful for it.

7

HOPI SONGPOEMS AND SONGS

THIS CHAPTER WILL SURVEY the structure of Hopi songpoems and other Hopi song types. It is essential to note that native poetry does not exist in Hopi culture or in most other Native American cultures independent of the medium of music, and that music (with or without dancing) pervades almost every area of Hopi culture, as it does in most other Native American cultures. The focus of this chapter will be on the aspects of song and song-poem structure that are important in Hopi culture for determining genres and subgenres, the ways in which such structure is a known and conscious part of Hopi culture, and how the important structural aspects of these traditional forms relate to the context in which they are performed. Before considering Hopi music, it is crucial to consider the background of the study of native American music and to survey the style of Pueblo music in general. A more complete account of the historical development of southwestern Indian ethnomusicology is found in Frisbie (1977).

There are two genres of Hopi music: songs and songpoems. Songs are fixed in form and limited to particular activities (such as game songs, lullabies, songs embedded in stories, and esoteric songs used in kiva ceremonies). They are learned as a part of customary, everyday life or ceremony, always in the appropriate contexts. Songpoems, as vehicles of creative poetry, are the object of much conscious attention and elaboration, involving composition, rehearsal, and evaluation.

THE STUDY OF NATIVE AMERICAN MUSIC
The study of Native American music began in 1882 (Baker 1978 [1882])

with a doctoral dissertation at Leipzig that dealt with the music of the Seneca, Ioway, Sioux, and other groups. The premise of the study reflects anthropological debate of the time: "the Indian, in order to give expression to the same feelings as civilized man, must also make the same choice of tonalities" (Baker 1978:48). Baker asserted that Native Americans possessed scales comparable to those of Western music. This idea was based upon the belief that humanity everywhere shared the same mental essentials. Despite this relativistic position, the study of Native American music was in fact guided by Social Darwinism. This theoretical stance posited a gradual development from "primitive" cultures to "civilized" ones. Humanity everywhere had the same musical instincts; the evolution of music would proceed, at whatever pace, in the same direction. Scholars (and the lay public) believed that human cultures evolve just like any other phenomena in the natural world. The logical progression of music was from a primeval impulse to express emotion by means of rhythm with a monotone pitch (Fillmore 1896:274), adding other pitches until a five-tone (pentatonic) had been achieved. The music of preliterate peoples thus constituted more of a living museum than an anthropological laboratory.

Some early observers, despite their intellectual motivations, learned to enjoy the music they heard. Natalie Curtis Burlin, in reacting to Hopi music, stated that even though "the last element of music to evolve [harmony]" was lacking (1907:vi), their "music astounded me. I felt I had come in search of gold [an old theme in southwestern exploration!] and found diamonds" (1903:627).

Another early observer, Jesse W. Fewkes, also appreciated Hopi music: "I wish everyone who has not heard the best in aboriginal music could hear the songs of the Flute festival" (quoted in Hough 1897:163). As alluded to above, however, the study of Native American music was caught up in a theoretical debate as to whether it exhibited any organization comparable to the Western scale (McNutt 1984), Most scholars posited a natural harmonic scale identical to the chromatic scale of Western music, which they considered to be innate. Benjamin Gilman (1891), the only major opponent of this idea, held that the tonal organization of Native American music was entirely learned. For Gilman, the unit of preliterate musical organization was melodic sequences; no evidence of scalar organization was to be found. His evidence for this was that the tones of one song do not match the tones of other songs, and that the tonal array of each song of his samples of Hopi and Zuni music was unique (1908:9). In his analysis of Zuni music, he stated that the melodies were "songs without scale" and denied the existence of a "sense of scale" on the part of Zuni musicians (Gilman 1908:9). In his companion study of Hopi music, Gilman concluded that "[the] evidence of the present notations bears strongly against the diatonic [scalar] theory of this [Native American] music" (1908:5).

Gilman compared Native American music with other non-Western musical traditions in a state-of-the-art paper, "The Science of Exotic Music" (Gilman 1909), published in *Science*, which at the time was a popular magazine like *Scientific American* is today. In his summary, he stated that non-Western music is anharmonic: "As far as is known, true harmony [the use of groups of tones, or **tone clusters**, to support melodic pitches that are related by degree of scale] does not exist outside of European music" (1909:533). The lack of harmony is compensated for by a more complex rhythmic structure (1909:534). The division of sound waves into scales (where the notion of scale exists) varies across cultures. Melody also varies cross-culturally (1909:534), though the idea of a **tonic** ("one note distinguished as the principal one," 1909:533) is universal. In arguing for a culturally defined basis of music, Gilman single-handedly began what was to remain the central debate in the field for decades.

Reaction to Gilman at the time was dogmatic. Most scholars held fast to the belief that the trichotomy of rhythm, melody, and harmony echoed the Social Darwinian stages of Savagery, Barbarism, and Civilization. They found it necessary to posit an innate, universal scale that was the basis for all music in the world, despite repeated evidence to the contrary in their own writings. Fillmore (1894), for example, while insisting that Tiwa, Zuni, Hopi, and Navajo music used a pentatonic scale and implied Western harmony, had to admit that "a still more puzzling phenomenon remained in the presence of a *considerable* number of songs the tone of which could not be referred to any one scale" (Fillmore 1894:618; emphasis added). Here is candid admission that his theory in fact did not work.

In a study of twenty-eight Navajo songs collected by Washington Matthews (Fillmore 1897), the pitch arrays of only six of the total sample, 21 percent, actually fit Fillmore's prescribed scales. The assumption that the basis of Native American music was comparable to the underlying pitch system of Western music was to persist to a surprising extent through the succeeding decades.

Gilman (1909) also recognized the importance of cultural variation in the study of music, including differing emotional responses to music.

The comparative method used by Social Darwinists (ca. 1880–1910), however, conveniently ignored the cultural context of music. Only the linguistic text (if any) and melody were studied (McLeod 1974:104) in order to produce a description of the style of a particular music that would fit into general schemes of culture history. Early concern for Pueblo (and other Native American) music in context was usually limited to blanket statements about the pervasive use of song and dance in native ceremonial life; for example, Fewkes noted that "smoking, singing and praying impart to the prayer-bearers the will of the worshippers" (1902:504). Often ethnographers also noted that music accompanied nearly all aspects of native life (see Curtis 1903:626, for example). The only detailed cultural analyses of Native American songs were observations about the poetics of the texts. For example, Densmore stated that certain songs from Santo Domingo Pueblo had thirty to fifty lines in translation, telling a story with shifts in point of view (1950:456–57). Not until the 1950s, however, would the study of music in its social context and the poetics of Native American songs claim serious theoretical interest.

PUEBLO MUSICAL STYLE

George Herzog was the first to state that "The melodies of the Pueblos in New Mexico and Arizona are among the most complex melodies known" in the Americas (1935:23). Data accumulated by 1950 led Nettl to state definitively that "the style of the Pueblos is the most complex in North America," with greater complexity among the Western Pueblos (Keresans, Zunis, Hopis) than among the Eastern Pueblo [Tanoan] cultures (Nettl 1954:30). A sizable body of published scholarly transcription of Pueblo music exists: Gilman (1891, 1908), Curtis (1903, 1906, 1907, 1921), Spinden (1917, 1931), Jeancon (1924), H. Roberts (1927, 1928), Herzog (1936; material in Evans and Evans 1931), Densmore (1938, 1957), MacLeish (1941), Van Stone (1941), Kurath (1957, 1962, 1965), Kurath and Garcia (1969), and Rhodes (1972, 1977). For the history of the study of southwestern and particularly Pueblo music, see H. Roberts (1927) and D. Roberts (1972).

The most important single statement about Pueblo musical style is still Herzog (1936; though Kurath and Garcia 1969 and B. Tedlock 1980 provide amplification), but the first published work on Pueblo music was Helen Roberts's analysis of the Picuris contes-fables that had been gathered by John Peabody Harrington (H. Roberts 1928). The analysis was of the scale-seeking school (even Herzog looked for scales). Roberts insisted that there were "ordinary scales in these Picuris songs" (1928:400), but had to admit that there are "pitches [in the songs] which do not coincide with those of our diatonic or chromatic scales" (1928:339). Her explanation for the nonscalar pitches is that they serve as ornamentation: they "supplement them [the basic notes of the scale], enriching the melodic color" (1928:400); a few pages later, however, she states that there is little in the way of ornamentation (1928:414). Every major study of Pueblo music thereafter (until the work of List discussed below) clung to the idea of scales in Pueblo music, while often furnishing evidence to the contrary (Herzog 1936; H. Roberts 1936a, 1936b; Chesky 1941; Nettl 1954; Kurath 1965; Kurath and Garcia 1969).

If Gilman was right about Pueblo music being nonscalar, how, then, does the Pueblo composer think about pitches? What relation do they have to each other? Is there a single keynote (tonic) in Pueblo music or are there several? It seems that some principal pitches may be altered for aesthetic purposes, especially during latter portions of a piece of music. Is the relationship of two different pitches (the interval between them) the dynamic tension in the practice? To consider these questions, we must consider form (melodic shape and musical phrases), and to do that, we must in turn consider rhythm.

Rhythm, the neglected stepchild of the early ethnomusicology of Native America, is just as variable in Pueblo music as the tonal materials. Most scholars assumed **meter** (in Western music a regular rhythmic pattern repeated throughout an entire piece of music, with one primary beat per repetition of the rhythmic unit) to be present in Pueblo music along with the nonexistent scales. Again, their own transcriptions betray them. Helen Roberts, for example, in her analysis of Picuris narrative songs, reports that "absolute metric regularity was not found in any song" (1928:413). Nearly all published transcriptions of Pueblo music (in Western musical notation), in fact, show alternating, nonperiodic rhythm.

Herzog (1936) was the first to provide a correct analysis of the rhythmic structure of Pueblo music. He found that the fundamental beat pattern (duple) is used to create rhythmic motifs and phrases that are employed more or less freely (1936:292). He claimed that the greatest rhythmic tension was at the section boundaries of Pueblo songs. To add variety, a rhythmic unit may be expressed in less time than when it was first heard (**diminution**), it may be drawn out (**augmentation**), the basic pulsation (duple or triple) may be briefly shifted (**hemiola**), or the speed (**tempo**) may be varied (1936:292–93).

Thus, Pueblo music is not metrical in the Western sense. It has a basic duple beat, to which the rhythm of the melody is set, though independent rhythmic motifs may be inserted for aesthetics or genre requirements. There may be interaction between the two levels of rhythm (fundamental and melodic), especially at the beginning and end of songs or their major sections. Not surprisingly, Tewas (Garcia and Garcia 1968:240; Kurath and Garcia 1969:88), Zunis (B. Tedlock 1980:28–29), and Hopis have technical terms for discussing and evaluating rhythmic units and song sections.

The heart of the issue of what actually makes up Pueblo music is the matter of **form**. The basic musical unit is the **phrase** (a sequence of pitches and its associated rhythm), which has both melodic and rhythmic properties. Synonyms for *musical phrase* include *period* and *melodic contour*. Parts of a phrase may be conveniently termed as *motives*. For purposes of analysis, musical phrases are symbolized by capital letters, and motives are represented by lower case letters.

The basic phrasal structure of Pueblo music is AABBA (Herzog 1936:291; Densmore 1938:32; Nettl 1954:32). This basic form is made up of smaller units: in the Eastern Pueblos (Tanoan) three or four phrases are used, with repetition, in the Western Pueblos (Keresans, Zunis, Hopis) subphrases are more motivic, with "ten or twelve different melodic fragments sung progressively" (Chesky 1941:12). In the music of the Western Pueblos, there are two distinct halves (AA and BB), each with its own tonality (Herzog 1936:292; Kurath 1959, 1960, 1965; Kurath and Garcia 1969:99–100; B. Tedlock 1980:16–21). Introductions, connecting interludes, and formal endings (**codas**) are common in all Pueblo musics, Herzog noted; all these parts are centered primarily on the tonic, but in the Western Pueblos the coda may be centered around a tone slightly higher (1936:242).

HOPI MUSICAL STYLE

As mentioned above, Hopi musical practice distinguishes two main sung genres: songpoems, whose complex structure is described by a developed terminology; and songs, which are simple in form, fixed in structure, and learned as a part of folklore or ritual. It is the structure of songpoems that will concern us here. The salient structural features of Hopi songpoems concern sections and phrases, elements of musical form, and the paired melodic contours and associated rhythms of both. Subgenres of songpoems are distinguished by specific melodic and rhythmic pattern, vocables, and sometimes instrumental accompaniments.

Rhodes (1977:15–16) gives the following detailed anatomy of the Hopi songpoem:

> A = introduction
> a a' b b'
> ending section
> coda
>
> A' (repetition of A)
>
> B = different introduction
> c c' b b'
> ending section
> coda
>
> B (repeat of B)
>
> A" (recapitulation of A)

For social dances, rhythms are more complex (tempo changes for short periods; many pauses), and songpoems for social dances tend to have more vocables (Rhodes 1977:19–20).

George List notes that "[a]ll songs composed at the First Mesa are cased in a similar form" (1967:45):

> Full form = A A B B A
> A = x a y
> B = z b a y

Here, x is an introduction that identifies the song, that is, it functions as a genre signature. The y is an identifying coda to the first section, and z signals the beginning of the B section. The z identifier may contain the expression *hapi me'*, "verily hark" (List 1967:45). Concerning tonal materials used in Hopi songpoems,

> The partial change in the pitch of repeated phrases, which has already

been seen to resist explanation by modulation, is the most noteworthy formal feature of this music. . . . The change is of two kinds: a larger shift of about a semitone, which may affect any of the notes of a phrase, and which is illustrated in almost all of the melodies; and a smaller and less frequent shift of about a quarter tone, affecting only notes whose central position or office as starting points distinguishes them as axes or bases. . . . Simple mutation may terminate either by the return of the shifted notes, or the advance of others . . . (Gilman 1908:16–17).

Table 7.1 provides an overview of the Hopi terms for the parts of a songpoem.

TABLE 7.1. PARTS OF A HOPI SONGPOEM

atkyaqngwa'at	downward part
kuyngwa'at[a]	opening phrase (lit. "manifestation," sung twice)
tögngwa'at[b]	chorus (lit. "crying/shouting out," sung twice)
so'ngwa'at	refrain (lit. "ending," sung once)
	1. verse A
	2. verse A₁
omiwa'at	upward part
kuyngwa'at	opening phrase (sung twice)
tögngwa'at	chorus (sung twice)
so'ngwa'at	refrain (sung once)
	3. verse B
	4. verse B₁
atkyaqngwa'at	downward part
kuyngwa'at	opening phrase (sung twice)
tögngwa'at	chorus (sung twice)
so'ngwa'at	refrain (sung once)
	5. verse A₂
tootsi[d]	coda (lit. 'shoe')

a. Identifies subgenre; at this point the songpoem becomes recognizable.
b. Contains main poetic message.
c. Sums up message of "chorus."
d. Used only in social dance songs.

The *tootsi,* 'shoe/coda,' is used only in social dance songs. Both the downward part and the upward parts have the same three sections, which are as follows, but the *töqngwa'at* in the upward part is usually more elaborate.

kuyngwa'at	opening phrase (sung twice)
töqngwa'at	chorus (sung twice)
so'ngwa'at	refrain (sung once)

The *kuyngwa'at* means literally 'manifestation'; it is at this point that the song becomes recognizable and that identifies its subgenre. The *töqngwa'at* is usually translated as 'chorus' because the main poetic message is contained in this part; the singers "sing out" (the word literally means 'a crying/shouting out') the message as a "chorus." The refrain (*so'ngwa'at*) means literally 'ending' and might be more conventionally translated into English as a coda, but the folk translation 'refrain' captures the notion that this section (often consisting of vocables) sums up the message of the "chorus."

It takes only a few rehearsals to insure a perfect kachina performance, because "there are fixed dance routines and song rhythms for each type of impersonation, so that knowledge of the tune pattern carries with it the clues to the proper gestures and steps" (Titiev 1944:127, n. 196). The names for the songpoem parts are used not only in rehearsal, but also in evaluation. See the songpoem presented in chapter 8 for example of each part.

Further variety is afforded by rhythmic complexity; the most common is a momentary shift from duple to triple rhythm (hemiola), rhythmic figures used as motifs within a musical phrase (syncopation, various dotted rhythms, and others), tempo changes (largely within a phrase or section), and pauses placed largely at the ends of phrases and sections. Such rhythmic variety suggests that Hopi songpoems are sectioned into melodic contours associated with textual and rhythmic material, and that this organization is psychologically real.

List, in two seminal papers, has shown that this is indeed the case. "The Hopis conceive melody as a series of contours rather than as a series of discrete pitches (List 1987:23). Citing Gilman's work (published in 1908, but done in the early 1890s): "After employing several methods of transcription, including that of attempting to establish microtones [quarter tones and less], he [Gilman] came to the conclusion that Hopi melody is without a scale" (List 1987:23). In five versions of the same Hopi kachina song, List was unable to find the same discrete pitches. While the melodic contours remain the same, no two versions are exactly alike in terms of the precise relationships among the pitches.

List (1987) used different versions of the same lullaby to the same effect; despite a similarity in melodic contour, there was no exact similarity in the actual sequence of pitches. As in the previous case, the melodic contour retains its distinctive character, and this is how Hopi and other Pueblo Indians recognize, learn, and process melody.

Similar results are found in Laguna (Keresan) and Zuni musical form. B. Tedlock observes that the three kinds of Zuni kachina songs have characteristic melodic contours (1980:26). Roberts (1936b) did the same type of analysis, transcribing two Laguna and one Zuni version of the same Chakwena kachina song. She did not explicitly come to the same conclusion about the primacy of contours over ranked sets of individual pitches.

Curtis (1903) gives additional evidence for the unity of the songpoem's melodic-rhythmic whole. When in the field, a Hopi volunteered to sing her a song that he had composed. After recording it, she asked him about the composition process.

> "Did you make the words first and then the music, or how was it?" I asked. The Indian looked puzzled, as though not understanding the question. Then he said, simply "I do not make first words, then music. I make a *song* [emphasis in original]. My song has words and music. (Curtis 1903:631)

This, of course, is what Gilman had proposed all along: "These musicians do not seem to grasp the notes they utter as steps in any scale at all, but simply as constituents in a familiar sequence of tones, unrolling itself from memory." (Gilman 1909:534)

The parts of a songpoem (section, phrase) have, of course, names which are used to discuss the form and esthetics of a piece when necessary or desirable. (The reader is referred to Table 7.1 above for the detailed Hopi terminology used for this purpose.) Thus, we may accept Hopi songpoems as a nonscalar music in which melodic contours are the basic units, with tension created by intervals (Herzog's idea), melodic highlighting (the raising of pitches), and varying rhythmic figures to create the variety that is the substance of this art.

Another way in which discrete parts of songpoems are cognitively real to Hopis and other bearers of Pueblo cultures is the salience of genre signatures. List (1962:32) noticed that Hopis could identify the type of song even if they had not heard it before. B. Tedlock (1980:26) noted that the three kinds of Zuni kachina songs are distinguished by characteristic melodic contours. In Tewa songpoems, differing monotone introductions and codas are typical of different song types (Kurath 1965), and shifts of tempo depend on the dance genre (and hence the songpoem type; Kurath and Garcia 1969:88). In addition to variations of melodic contour, introduction, coda, and typical tempo shifts, Hopi songpoem practice also makes use of **vocables** typical of a given genre of music. Certain rhythmic figures also are typical of particular genres.

Performance practice relates the Hopi songpoem to actual contexts of performance. The full-throated singing and low pitch of Pueblo men's singing is noted in almost every description of Pueblo music (see for example, Nettl 1954:30–31). Yet an underlying ideal of moderation is evident in Pueblo musical practice. For example, in distinguishing Pueblo from Plains music, Kurath states that "The [Tewa] singing is neither shrill nor subdued, simply mezzo forte" (1969:515). This full-throated, resonant moderation carries over even to Tewa adaptation of social dances to commercial, exhibition performances:

> Until recently all Ceremonial judges were Anglos, setting up a conflict between two aesthetic systems. In dance competitions the Anglo judges were primarily concerned with costumes and "pep." On the other hand, when the Tewa evaluate a dance performance, they are more concerned with the song composition and a conservative, solemn, demure, uniform dance style. The group should move as one organism with no overtly energetic individual standing out. (Sweet 1983:257)

This ideal of moderation in performance is also present in Hopi practice. Although each type of kachina music has its own style, the ideal is a restrained manner of singing, not a rollicking, "jamboree" style.

MUSIC AND SOCIOCULTURAL CONTEXT

Music is part of daily life for the Hopis.

> Song is an integral part of the culture. It serves in religious ceremonies;

it cures the sick; it accompanies dance, game or work; it soothes the infant. It is a didactic force. A song is rarely sung purely for entertainment . . . older Hopis sing to their children and grandchildren, partly for their entertainment, and partly to develop a loyalty to the culture. (List 1962:30)

As another writer notes:

It is well nigh impossible to conceive of the importance of song in the life of the Hopi. To him, song is the breath of the spirit that consecrates the acts of life. Not all songs are religious, but there are few tasks, light or heavy, scarcely an event great or small without its fitting song . . . They never seem to tire of singing. (Williams 1948:71)

And songs are often sung to oneself while working or traveling. (In the following passage, the word *taawi* refers to both songs and songpoems, because of the common medium.)

Hopi hiita hintsakninik pam taawit akw enang hiita hintsakngwu. Me, taaqa hisat pasminen tawkyangwnigwu. Pam yaw uuyiy navotnaniqe oovi tawkyangw pangso pitutongwu, aasavo yaw puma havivokyalniqat oovi. Pu' pam pang waynumkyangw piw tawkyangwngwu.

Noq pu' wuuti, maana piw ngumante' pam taawit akw enang ngumantangwu. . . . Taawit akw yaw put tumala'at pay qa pas maqsoniningwu . . .

Noq pu' wuuti piw tiy puupuwvitsne' pam piw put aw puwvitstawit tawlawngwu.

Noq pu' hakim tsaatsayom nen hakim hohonaqye' hakim piw naat pay taawit akw enang hohonaqyangwu.

Pu' piw hakim momoryaqw pep pu' piw naat suukya taawiningwu. Pu' hikis piw nukpana it hiita tuskyaptawit piw maskya'yta . . . Pu' soosoy himu wiimi taawita akw pasiwta . . .

Noq pu' sosotukwyaqam piw pas naap taatawi'yyungwa. Puma pantsatsyaqam put tawkyaakyangw nanavö'yangwu . . .

Noq pu' paasat I' tuutuwutsi as hisat pay sumataq pas sonqa taawi'ytangwu . . .

Pu' Hopi yaw pay yaapaniiqe oovi qa suukw hiituy lavayiyamuy ang enang yeewatima. Niiqe oovi ephaqam himuwa taawi Si'olalvayngwu pu' piw Tasaplalvayngwu. Pu' pay aapiy piw himusinmuy lavayi'am hiita taawit pay pas son ep qa pakiwtangwu. Pu' pay peehu taatawi pay pas hisat-tatawiniqw oovi pay peehu kur hiita lalvayya. (Lomatuwa'yma et al. 1994:476)

∅

In the past a Hopi did everything by means of a song. One sang on the way to the fields so that his plants would know he was on his way, and be awake upon his arrival. One also sang as one walked about the plants (hoeing and working).

A woman or girl would grind corn with a song. . . . By means of a song she would make the task less tedious . . .

A woman would put her child to sleep with a lullaby.

Playing as children, we would play by means of a song.

When one swims there is still another song.

Even the evil-doer has a witching song in reserve . . .

All ceremonies are complete only with songs . . .

The guessing games players had their own songs. Those who played sang as they competed . . .

Now then, it seems as if stories almost always had a song to them . . .

The Hopi is a mockingbird because he makes up songs in the languages of different people. One song might be in Zuni, and yet another in Navajo. Moreover, some Native American language is contained in every song. Some songs are such old songs that their language is obscure.

The named kinds of Hopi songs and songpoems include the following:

maktawi	hunting song
natwàntawi	field song
ngumantawi	grinding song
puwtawi	lullaby
pastawi	hoeing song
powatawi	curing song
sosotukwtawi	gambling song
tsakotawi	children's song
tsovalàntawi	harvesting song
tuwutstawi	story song *(conte-fable)*
uytawi	planting song
wúngwìntawi	plant growing song

As their names imply, most of these songs accompany traditional eco-
nomic activities. The supernatural effectiveness of song is implicit in "everyday" songs.

> Maktawiy akw tuutuvosiptuy amumi suyan unangway màatakne pumuy
> tuyqawvangwu.
>   If he reveals a good heart to the game animals by means of his own
> hunting song, he wins them over.

Ordinary activities could be occasions for savoring songpoems. There
were grinding parties where men or boys sang (Stephen 1936:153–54), but
such activities were not appropriate when war was planned, as it made
the ground soft and moist, and snow and frozen ground was desired (Parsons
1925:16). During the winter, however, when a man had several fleeces
he wanted to process (formerly, a Hopi man provided all the textiles for
his family), he would have the kiva chiefs announce a spinning party,
whereby all men interested in helping would gather in the man's kiva
and spin while singing kachina songs, with elders and notable singers
correcting.

The only subgenres in the list that seem to be nearly devoid of supernatural force are lullabies and the children's songs which accompany games
or have gestures that go along with the words. Lullabies, though few in
number (see Sands and Sekaquaptewa 1978) are very significant in the
culture. In addition to *puwtawi*, there are also songs called *puwvitstawi*,
'arriving at sleep song,' and *titaptawi*, 'baby-sitting song.'

Songpoems composed for public performances include *tseletawi*,
'social dance songs,' *tsukutawi*, 'clown songs,' used by clowns in their
public performances, and *katsintawi*, 'kachina songs.' Social dance songpoems are used in January (Buffalo Dance, Eagle Dance) and in July
or August (Butterfly Dance), with kachina songpoems being performed
in the intervening growing season. Another kind of public performance
involves girls, boys, or members of a women's society canvassing door-
to-door for food. Such a group will sing a *suspaltawi*, 'begging song.'
Most songpoems are composed by men, but some may be made by
women for the Basket Dances (September, October) which are presented
by the women's societies.

Events at which social and kachina songpoems are performed include
most of the following sequence of songs:

yungtawi	'kiva entering song'
awtawi	'processional song'
eptawi	'arrival song'
tiitawi	'dance song'
hoyoktawi	'moving song'
nimàntawi	'recessional song'

The entering song is sung inside the kiva prior to the public perform-ance. The processional song accompanies the dancers to the plaza, and the arrival song is sung in place once they arrive. The songpoem for the dance itself is performed three times in the plaza (on the northwest, south-west, and southeast sides; a plaza is open to the northeast). A moving song may accompany them as they shift position. The recessional is sung as the performers leave the plaza. Most public performances do not have each songpoem of this sequence, however.

The religious societies have ritual songs (*wimtawi*) that are esoteric, known only to their group and members of the clan that controls or "owns" the ceremony. These are sung only in the appropriate context (usually the kiva). They include the following:

makwàntawi	asperging song
navòotsiwtawi	purification/discharming song
ngáakùytawi	ritual song
pahotsöqa'atstawi	prayer stick making song
pavasìwtawi	ritual prayer song
wángwaytawi	cloud-summoning song

Ritual songs trace the mythical history of the migration of the control-ling clan to Hopi. The words of esoteric songs are terse and cryptic; one must know the myth to understand their imagery. As a group, they form a song cycle that is related to the ritual they encode and actuate.

Three religious societies have a form restricted primarily to their own usage, the *tawsoma*, 'song-tie.' This satirizing in songs is used in the pub-lic performance of the Maraw, Singers, and Wuwutsim Societies. The male Singers and Wuwutsim make fun of the female Maraw members in their public performance in November. The following January, the women reciprocate. In the song-tying of these societies, individuals may be mentioned by name; such direct public criticism is unparalleled in

Pueblo cultures. Other kinds of song may also be satirical. Lyrics for a Buffalo Dance song, for example, may song-tie particular social conditions or attitudes. In a broader reading, song-tying may mean any specific mention in a song of satirical, spiritual, or historical significance.

Hopi music is usually happy and uplifting. A common complaint about Anglo music is that it is love-sick and sad for a variety of reasons.

> A Hopi woman told me that her children incessantly play popular records. Of the singers on these records, she complained. "They are always sobbing and crying. Their heart is always breaking. I don't see how they can sing when their heart is breaking. I couldn't sing if my heart was breaking!" (List 1964:47)

A Hopi colleague once remarked to me, upon hearing the refrain of a Linda Ronstadt song ("You're no good, you're no good, you're no good . . ."), "How can one hope for rain with such a negative attitude?" (It was the rainy season in Tucson). Hopi music is positive in force. One should maintain a positive attitude while singing. The word *Hopi* means "of positive attitude and commensurate behavior," so Hopis must exercise control over their thoughts and emotions; one must have a 'good heart' (*nukwangw'unangwa'yta*).

> A "good heart" means that one must not feel fear, anger, sadness, or worry. In other words, one must be inwardly tranquil and of good will.

It is interesting to note in this connection that the Hopi use the same word (*naawakna*) for 'to will' and 'to pray.' Praying is willing. (Thompson and Joseph 1944:41)

The attitude of positive moderation affects performance practices; one should not sing with gusto or verve. Putting one's heart into one's singing means whole-hearted concentration, but not complete abandon. A metaphysics similar to that of Hopi culture (will and its verbal expression can effect reality) is shared by other Pueblo cultures; the Acoma poet Simon Ortiz comments that "a song is made substantial by its context — that is its reality that which is there and what is brought about by the song" (S. Ortiz 1977:6).

There are potentially two genres of Hopi music: songs and songpoems. Songs, which are fixed in form and limited to particular activities (game songs, lullabies, songs embedded in stories; esoteric songs that are used in kiva ceremonies). They are learnt as a part of folklore or ceremony, in the appropriate contexts. The songpoems, as vehicles of poetry, are the object of much cognitive activity in the sociocultural context (compositional process, rehearsal and evaluation).

It is important to remember that traditional Pueblo literature is anchored in place. It describes or refers to the local milieu. This localization is symbolic. "It might be said that the Tewa, by defining periodically among *what* they move [the village boundaries and shrines] reaffirm *who* they are" (A. Ortiz 1969:155; emphasis in original).

The Pueblo Indians use memory as a library; the narrated word, the sung word, the ritual word all have a special, spatial quality. Each localizes the tradition and relates it to those present. Moreover, the act of pronouncing words is believed to have supernatural efficacy. To say something or sing about it is to bring it about. In this way the verbal arts of the Pueblo cultures are significant in a way that they are not in Western literature.

A Hopi song or songpoem is symbolic of place. The poetry of a songpoem is enveloped by the accompanying musical texture (melody and rhythmic articulation); the songpoem as a whole is then encapsulated in an actual context of performance, whether an individual singing to his corn plants or the singing at a plaza dance.

The Hopi songpoem uses the AABBA form noted above; the greatest pitch range and most complex rhythms occur at the beginning of each B section. The words of the B section are the most suggestive to Hopis, and it is this portion of the lyric that is the most open to differing interpretation by Hopis (Shaul 1992). In other words, the most elaborate music envelopes and highlights the most semantically pregnant text. Recognizing different named genres of songpoems and segmenting melodic contours (*tawvö*, 'song path'; compare *tawvötavi*, 'song style,' literally 'the way the song path is set') is the basis of Hopi musical practice (composition, aesthetic evaluation, rehearsal, and performance). It is the conscious ability to segment the music that allows for the semantic and musical highlight at the start of the B section.

This semiotic node is thus the center of the songpoem, which is firmly anchored in Hopi culture. The songpoem's complex form, its context, and its holism are all crucial elements in understanding the genre.

A good introduction to the nature of Hopi musical contexts is provided by the four common lullabies.

all Hopi lullabies are meant to pacify . . . They are similar in structure: in each the animal [the lullaby is about] is identified, a particularized location is defined, and the action is then described. Both [the description and the action] remain in the present tense throughout and have only one voice, the singer's. (Sands and Sekaquaptewa 1978:198)

Two of the lullabies are soothing, but two are threatening: in the Owl Lullaby, owls are looking for those who are cry-babies and whiners. This contrasts markedly with the Stinkbug Lullaby in which the randomness of movement and general passivity of the Hopi baby are emphasized. Not only are the words (and vocables: *veveve*, for example) soporific, but they also have cultural content. They are a primer about the role of the individual in a collective culture: "Hopi culture is cooperation without surrender" (E. Sekaquaptewa in *Hopi: Songs of the Fourth World*).

Songs are learned orally, by rote (*tawkosi*, 'learn a song/learn orally'). Song composition is referred to by the term *yeewa*, 'creative plan/idea,' and the production of new songpoems is a cultural ideal.

> Itam pas qa tawsakwit akwya; itam pas yeewat akwya.
> We're not using a used-up song, but instead a fresh one.

The word for a song that has already been performed in public (*tawsakwi*) means literally that the song is 'broken down' or 'worn out,' implying that the song is stale and therefore undesirable for further public scrutiny.

After one composes a songpoem, it is "revealed" to a group of people.

> Haqawa kya yeewa'ataqa put tsìikyaknani.
> Whoever has a new song, crack it open.

The idea of "cracking open" idiomatically underscores the unveiling, the revelation of one's creativity to a group of potential performers. A song which gains acceptance is then rehearsed. The notion of rehearsal is an extended sense of *wuuwa*, 'think/ponder.' The entire fabric of the songpoem (melody, rhythm, lyrics) is considered as the group edits the contribution.

The conventional imagery of Hopi songpoems is intimately tied to the culture. One common metaphor in Hopi songpoems involves corn ("people are corn," as evidenced by such statements as *um hapi qaa'öniwti*, 'you will become corn'; M. Black 1984:279). Corn, like humans, is born, takes sustenance, has eyes (*poosi*, 'seeds,' also means 'eyes'), and at death leaves behind an empty form (*qatungwu*; M. Black 1984:280–82). Corn, however, is more specifically female, since it is life-bearing: the plants are *uuyi maanatu*, 'plant maidens,' or *qaa'ö maanatu*, 'corn maidens,' *paavönmanatu*, 'shower maidens,' or *humisimanatu*, 'seed corn maidens,' that enjoy (*heveveta*) a cool rain shower, just like humans (M. Black 1984:283–85). When the corn ears develop, the plant is said to have come to have children (*timu-yva*), the ears being her children (*timat*), and in general, "corn is our mother" ([*qaa'ö pas pay itangu*]; M. Black 1984:286), an icon of the female creative force and matrilineality in Hopi culture.

In a similar vein, there are other important cultural themes in Hopi songpoems: the rain complex, being happy, prayers, and being grateful.

> Hin sen itanam
> umumi lávaytoti.
> "Owii'."
> "Owii, yaw iitam
> paayoyangwu
> suvuuyoyangwu
> aqw iitam
> ookwatuwyani."

> 𝄇

> What did your fathers
> pray of to you?
> "Yes."
> "Yes, with
> moist rains
> drizzle rains,
> that we
> humbly fulfill
> their prayers." (Kabotie, ed. 1978:23)

In this short extract of a songpoem by Dawakema, the important Hopi themes of humility, reciprocity, and moisture are all mentioned.

The songpoems are rooted in an expansive sociocultural context. They are literature at the highest level in terms of poetic use of language. There are several successive contexts in which a songpoem may exist. First of all, there is the composer's mind. Second of all, there is the rehearsal-editing context of the kiva. Thirdly, there are one or more public per-formances; and finally a songpoem may stick in anyone's mind for future use and savoring. As public art, songpoems are completely context ori-ented, although they are not necessarily context sensitive (see below).

David McAllester states that composition, "a constant process in Pueblo music" (1961:7), is the usual source of music. This contrasts with some Native American musical practices, in which songs are given in dreams, visions, or otherwise not consciously composed. Ruth Bunzel noted that Zuni kachina songs are composed anew for each dance (1932:495). For Keresan Deer and Buffalo dances at Cochiti, new songs are composed for every occasion (Kurath 1958:149). "In special [Cochiti] dance songs, the melodies are said to have remained unchanged through the years, though the words are revised each year. In other dances, neither the melody nor the words can be changed" (Lange 1959:311).

Kurath (1959:539) notes that Deer and Buffalo songs at Cochiti are always new, and that in Cochiti there are men known for their excellence in musical composition. In Zuni practice, "not just everyone can compose a song" (B. Tedlock 1980:21); a *tenaa washeyen'ona,* 'song composer,' is one with *tse'mak 'anikwa,* a 'smart mind or good memory.' Songs may also be borrowed from other pueblos or tribes (B. Tedlock 1980:24).

In Hopi musical practice, songpoem composition is a constant source of aesthetic enjoyment for both composers (*yeewa*), performers, and audi-ences, who are passive participants in any public performance.

> All adult [Hopi] males are members of the *kachina* cult and may there-
> fore compose *kachina* dance songs. Some men are more interested in
> composing these songs than others, and certain men in particular have
> developed a reputation for their skill in this art. Most Hopi men seem
> conscious of the stylistic factors which characterize *kachina* dance songs
> as well as those which differentiate one type of *kachina* dance song from
> another, but not all can verbalize these concepts. (List 1967:44)

Song styles change over time, due both to internal evolution of song styles and through extensive borrowing from other Native American groups, but Hopis can readily identify the types of song (List 1962:32–33), and com-posers must follow the genre conventions.

The amount of composition in Hopi musical life is extensive: for a night (kiva) dance, each kiva group needs two or three songs, and for a plaza dance twelve to sixteen new songs must be composed (Rhodes 1977:16), with the dance sponsor formally retaining composers. Since the Hopi songpoem is a public art, rehearsal is needed before performances, which in turn involves a gradual process of evaluation.

> Once the composer of the song has it firmly in mind, he will sing it to others in the kiva. There the others will learn it and contribute to it. If there are uncomfortable spots either in music or text, they will make suggestions for changes. . . . Such group participation in the compositional process is in no way regarded as a correction of the composer . . . it is thought of as the natural process any song must go through in order to have the right feeling. (Rhodes 1977:16)

The rehearsal-evaluative process at other pueblos is similar. Once in the kiva at Cochiti, "new melodies or words may be contributed by any kiva member" (Lange 1959:311). At Zuni, the rehearsal (*'itetcha*) is a process whereby the composer introduces his song, and it undergoes a process of group editing in which there is discussion and evaluation (B. Tedlock 1980:27). Collective editing of individual creativity reflects the Hopi collective orientation and ideal of moderation ("cooperation without surrender"). The resulting songpoem, as public art, fits into a public occasion (a dance), although it may be sung by individuals on other, private occasions. Within this notion of public occasion, however, there is no interaction between performer(s) and audience. The songpoem is a phenomenon unto itself; this is clear when one considers the actual structuring of the linguistic text and its relation to the musical envelope.

8

TOWARD A HOPI SONGBOOK

IN THIS CHAPTER, we will look at three Hopi songs and a songpoem. We will start with the simplest and increase in structural complexity.

The first song is the story song from the story "Coyote and the Birds" (chapter 4). This imitates the action of winnowing. The wording is simple: *pota* is the equivalent of spoken *poota*, 'coiled plaque basket'; *ini* is probably related to the root in the word *inta*, 'be contained'; *yowa* has no known meaning; *pu'* imitates the sound of the wind blowing away the chaff.

Melodically, there are two short motives ("A" and "B" in the transcription) that are repeated to form an AABB structure—a shape that is basic to Hopi music. (In this, and the other transcriptions, the pitches are a reasonable representation of the Hopi tonality.) A short coda of four pulses of indeterminate pitch end the piece.

fig 8.1

The next piece, perhaps the most cited piece of Hopi music, is the "Stinkbug Lullaby." For previous examples and treatments, see Curtis (1907 and 1921), MacLeish (1941), Sands and Sekaquaptewa (1978), and List (1993: chapter 4). The lyric is simple.

Puwva, puwva, puwva.
Hoohoyawu supöpave'e
naa'ikwìlkyango.

𝄢

Slept, slept, slept.
Stinkbugs—right on the road
carry each other on their backs.

Just as Hopi babies are carried about on the back of their mother or older sister (often in a shawl or quilt), stinkbugs will "hitch" rides with another stinkbug.

In the transcriptions of the lullaby below, the first one is a Third Mesa version; the second line is a transcription of a Second Mesa recording (List 1993:78–85).

The first line is set in a tonal contour that has two descents (each with the same characteristic rhythm [♪♫]), followed by a return to a pitch in-between the highest (starting) pitch and the lowest pitch.

fig 8.2

The next line (*hohoyawu supöpave'e*) always has a series of quick pulses on the same pitch with an upward skip and a tapering off that draws out the last syllable of *hohoyawu* (-*wu*). The first part of "right on the road" (*supö-*) has a stopping of airflow in both versions (represented by the symbol [♪ᵧ] in the transcriptions).

fig 8.3

The third line is fitted to a third repetition of the preceding rhythmic-melodic figure.

fig 8.4

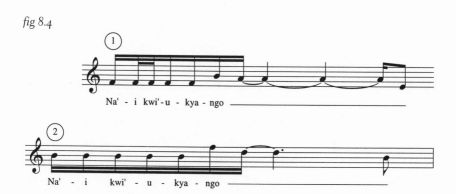

The final section returns to the first phrase. The first phrase ("A" in the transcription) may be repeated with elaboration on the soporific word *puwva*.

fig 8.5

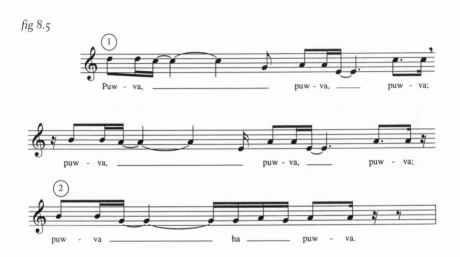

There may be a coda after the second A at the end (as in the first example here).

To sum up so far: Hopi song architecture is symmetrical, based on a two-phrase structure (AB) that may be repeated (AABB). The A phrase may be repeated or other music used to create a sense of ending. The rhythm is duple (groups of two or four pulses).

These basic traits are the basis of the elaborate songpoem form. Before turning to an example of this, we will look at an example of Hopi hymnody that validates the native Hopi song schema, changing the original tune. As in Bible translation, native form and rhetoric are used to legitimate new genres.

The hymn tune most widely known as "Flow Gently, Sweet Afton" is the basis of this example. In the transcription, the original tune is quoted in the upper line, with the Hopi melodic adaptation and lyric on the second (bottom) line. The Hopi text has stress marked (from the spoken language). One would expect that the musical stress (on the first pulse of each measure: ONE-two-three, waltz time) would coincide with linguistic stress. However, the two stress patterns do not coincide; they clash.

fig 8.6

Je   súst   u - ngwa - yát   akw i - tám tu' iw   yá

mok -

qéy   ep   i - tá   -   mu - ngem súw mun - gva   ná

197

fig 8.6 continued

God   aw

hàa - lay - ya - ní   pi   it Jé - sust ang'   á   soo - sok -

múy   sin - muy   a - mú - ngem   qa - tsit   aw   qe - ní

The original tune has three motives.

$$A = a_1\ a_2\ a_3\ a_4$$
$$B = b_1\ b_2\ c_1\ /\ a_3\ c_2$$

This means that phrase A has four variants of the same motive. Phrase B is made up of two variants of two motives.

Compare the original and Hopi versions.

model:	a_1	a_2	a_3	a_4	b_1	b_2	c_1	$/a_3$ c_2
Hopi:	a	a'	d	d'				

The Hopi version is half as long as the original tune, creating a two-part structure.

The Hopi lyric is as follows: the word stress has been written with an acute accent above the stressed vowel. Musical stress is marked above the text (there are four musical stresses per line).

<pre>
        /   /   /   /
Jésust ungwáyat akw ítam tú'iwya
        /   /   /   /
Mókqey ep itámungem súus múngvana
        /   /   /   /
Gód aw háalayyani, pi it Jésust áng'à
        /   /   /   /
sóosokmuy sínmuy amúngem qátsit aw qéni.
</pre>

If one groups the material in lines defined by the musical "stress," an eight-line structure is apparent, with strong beats on one and four (ONE-two-three-FOUR).

<pre>
                    /   /
Jé-   -sust ungwáyat
                      /   /
akw i-   -tám tú' iwya
                    /   /
mók-   -qey ep itá-
                              /
-mungem   súus múngvana
                      /   /
Gód aw   háalayyani
                    /   /
pi it   Jésust áng'à
                    /   /
sòosok-   -muy sínmuy amú-
                         /   /
-ngem qá-   -tsit aw qéni
</pre>

There are one or two syllables of material at the left that are extrametrical (they do not figure in placing the strong beats), and are provided for in the original tune by the up-beat (the few notes before the first complete measure of each line of music) at the beginning of each line.

In this arrangement, the effect of rhyme (which is alien to Hopi poetry, but an obvious feature of hymns) is created, as can be seen in the final syllables.

-yat
-ya
-ta
-na
-ni

-'a
-mu
-ni

This array not only imitates a salient characteristic of the model western hymn, it also creates a basic duple rhythm.

We may now compare the Hopi version (in the first line of the transcription) with the original tune.

*fig 8.*7

We now pass to the analysis of a Hopi songpoem. The two phrase form (AB) repeated with the A phrase as a coda (AABBA) and basic duple (two-beat) rhythm observed so far persist, with the elaboration and variation that distinguish this art form, the poetry that is native to Hopi culture. The words of Hopi songpoems occur with music, creating a closed text world. Missing are modals such as "perhaps" and "maybe" that would serve to tie them to the potentiality of the real world; they are linked to the world outside the text by reference to possible real world events ("it will rain," "it is raining"). The songpoem discussed here was collected by Natalie Curtis from a composer named Koianimptiwa (Curtis 1907:484–85). It is a Korosta Kachina songpoem. For more on the imagery of Hopi songpoems, see M. Black (1984) and Shaul (1992); for an earlier version of this discussion, see Shaul (1994).

The lines of the transcription are determined by pausalization or by conjunctive verbs endings (such as -*kyangw*, 'while/as,' in the first section. Recall the A₁A₂B₁B₂A'. Each of the sections has an introduction (*kuyngwa'at*), a verse (*töqngwa'at*), and possibly a refrain (*so'ngwa'at*). In the text below, the *kuyngwa'at*, which is the first line and consists of vocables, is repeated. The lines of the verse are grouped together, separated from the refrain.

Aha ha'a, ihi hi'i.

♩

Sikyavolimu,
humisimanatu
Talasiyamuyu pitsangwatimakyang

♩

tuvenangöyimani.

♩

Aha ha'a, ihi hi'i.

♩

Sakwavolimu,
morisimanatu
talasiyamuyu pitsangwatimakyang

🎵

tuvenangöyimani.

The return part (*piw atkyaqngwa'at*) is as follows. It consists of the *kuyngwa'at*, which introduces three verses (one of which is repeated); there is no refrain.

Aha ha'a, ihi hiyi.

🎵

Humisimanatu
amunawita
tatangayatu tökiyuyuwintani.

🎵

Aha ha'a, ihi'i'i.

🎵

Morisimanatu
amunawita
tatangayaytu tökiyuyuwintani.

🎵

Aha'a'a, ihi'i'i.

🎵

Umu'u'uyi[y] amunawit yo'o'oy
yoy'umumutimani, tawanawita.

Here is a translation that is grouped by section ($A_1A_2 \ldots A'$) without attempting to reproduce the *kuyngwa'at* and the B sections which are also made up of vocables. The translation is as literal as possible for the convenience of the reader. The reader will find fuller exemplification in the musical example, particularly with the vocables.

Yellow butterfly
corn flower maidens

wearing their pollen on their faces as
they chase each other brightly along.

🎵

Blue butterfly
bean flower maidens
wearing their pollen on their faces as
they chase each other brightly along.

🎵

Along the line of
corn maidens
wasps hum along.

🎵

Along the line of
bean flower maidens
wasps hum along:

🎵

among your plants the rain
will go thundering rain all day long.

The imagery of rain is paramount and encompasses a double action: rows of growing corn or bean plants swaying in the cool breeze after a rain, and the line of girl dancers in a Butterfly Dance swaying with the music. Both the maturing plants and the girls are symbolic of late summer.

Several words deserve comment. The first is the verb *ngöyima*, 'go along chasing,' in the verse ending of A₁ and A₂. This verb is very similar in sound to the verb *ngu'yma*, 'go along grasping.' Both of these actions are suggested by the dancing girls and the swaying plants.

The word *taatangaya*, 'wasps,' has the collective suffix *-t* attached, suggesting various kinds of buzzing, social insects. Usually this is translated as "bees" (but cf. *momo*, 'bee'). Despite the carnivorous nature of wasps, the wasps here represent bees. The translation elicited by Curtis is "wild bees."

The Hopi lyric is embedded in a musical fabric. A transcription follows this discussion; readers may wish to refer to it to see how the lyric is combined with the musical text. Before discussing the relationship of the lyric to the music, it is necessary to consider the music itself. There is also a figure of the motives that make up the musical composition.

There is a fundamental duple rhythm articulated by at least a rattle or the tapping of a singer. Where there is a rest in the musical line, the percussive beat of the fundamental rhythm continues. The fundamental has been omitted in the transcription, as it is predictable.

fig 8.8

The *kuyngwa'at* is the genre signature of this kind of songpoem. It is rather plain, except for the very first instance and the first *kuyngwa'at* in the return section A'). Please refer to Figure 8.8; the *kuyngwa'at* is theme *x*. An A section (*atkyaq*) is the *kuyngwa'at* plus iterations of theme *a* (see Figure 8.9) plus the *so'ngwa'at* (theme *y*). The melodic contour *a* has a downward motion of a sixth (a fifth for variation in the A'), It is used in

fig 8.9

variants to articulate noun phrases, adverbial phrases, and verbs (lines of the lyric). After the initial statement of contour *a*, subsequent repetitions have syncopation. The verses (*töqngwa'at*) of A₁A₂ are not repeated as expected, but there are two additional verses in A.' The return section also uses a modulation of the upper thematic note (F# instead of G).

The *so'ngwa'at* theme *y* is similar in contour to the *kuyngwa'at*. This theme is used to articulate the final line of the lyric. The *so'ngwa'at* of the B sections is similar, and has the diagnostic vocable sequence *ayo linoya*. Instead of a *so'ngwa'at*, after the final verse of the return part (A', *piw atkyaqngwa'at*), there follows an extended coda (*tootsi*, literally "shoe") based on the melodic contours of the B sections.

The basic relationship between the lyric and music is that in the first sections (A₁A₂), the *töqngwa'at* articulates the lines of the verse, with the *so'ngwa'at* articulating the last line of the verse. The *a* and *b* melodic contours (see Figure 8.8) are fairly short, but varied by means of syncopation, the insertion of rests, dotted rhythms, and triple rhythmic figures. These additions simply draw out the syllable they co-occur with. Additional notes are also supplied as the final syllable of a line is drawn out on the end note the melodic contour (**pausalization**).

This discussion is incomplete; there is no treatment of the B sections, which consist entirely of music with vocables. Although it is incomplete, it is sufficient to show the relationship in the Hopi songpoem of the lyrics and their musical garb. Details, especially of rhythm and its relation to linguistic prosody (vowel length, falling tone in Third Mesa Hopi, glottal stops, pausals), remain to be investigated. The relationship of poetic imagery, as well as the aesthetics of vocables, have not been touched on. Clearly, this remarkable tradition remains critically unknown, and any full treatment will require the participation of native scholars and composers as well as interested outside investigators.

SKETCH OF HOPI GRAMMAR

IN EVERY HUMAN LANGUAGE, there are words that name entities (persons, things, animals, abstractions such as ideas or unicorns) and words that stand for actions or states of being. The entity naming words are called **nouns**, and the action/being words are called **verbs**. Consider the following Hopi sentence:

Sino	sikwit	tuumoyta.
person	meat	be eating

'The person is eating (the) meat.'

The verb in this sentence is *tuumoyta*, and it comes at the end of the sentence. The "do-er" (actor, entity doing the eating) is the noun *sino* 'person,' and the "do-ee" (the thing being eaten) is the noun *sikwi* 'meat.' The "do-er" is called the **subject** of the sentence, and the "do-ee" is called the **object**. Hopi sentences almost always have the following order: subject + object + verb (SOV). If there is no object, the order is: subject + verb.

Note that the object in the sentence above ends in -*t*. This ending is called an **objective**. It will be necessary in the glosses that face each selection in Hopi to refer to this type of marking: this will be done with the abbreviation **obj**.

The English language has words traditionally called prepositions. For example, the English word *to* is a preposition (Latin *pre*-, 'before,' + *position*) because it goes in front of the noun.

He went to the house.

In Hopi, the equivalent of prepositions are called **postpositions** (Latin *post*, 'after') because they follow the noun they go with.

Pam	sinot	aw	siivat	maqa.
s/he	person	to	money	gave.

'S/he gave money to the person.'

The Hopi equivalent of English *to* is the little word *aw*, which follows the noun (*sino*) it modifies. Notice that in this case the object (*siiva*, 'money') has the object marker, but that the word for "person" does as well. This is because "person" in this sentence is the **object of a preposition.**

There is another use for the objective marker. This is in indicating ownership. Consider the following sentence:

Pòoko	moosat	sikwiyat	tuumoyta.
dog	cat's	meat	be eating.

'The dog is eating the cat's meat.'

The owner (*moosa*, 'cat') has the objective ending. It is followed by the "owned" item (*sikwi*, 'meat') which also has an accusative marker attached (*-yat*, 'her/his/its,' obj.) because it is the object of the sentence.

In Hopi, a set of endings can be attached to verbs to indicate such ideas as 'while,' 'then,' and 'because.' These endings, in Hopi grammar, are called **modes.**

-kyangw	while/as
-t	then
-qe	because
-e'	if

When these endings are used, a second verb follows that has the same subject as the first verb, and the subject is not expressed again.

Pam	meloonit	tuumoyta-kyangw	wayma.
S/he	melon	eating-while	walking.

'S/he is eating melon while walking.'

Pam	tiimayi-t		nima.
S/he	watch dance-after		go home.

'S/he watched (the) dance and then went home.'

Pam	nima-qe	mangù'i.
S/he	go home-because	get tired.

'S/he went home because s/he got tired.'

Nu'	pangso	pit-'e	nösni.
I	to there	arrive-if	will eat.

'If I go there, I will eat.'

The mode endings are just like their English equivalents, except that they attach to the first verb instead of standing alone as single words.

The ending -kyangw has a plural form (-kyàakyangw); it is the only mode to have one.

Puma	meloonit	noonop-kyàakyangw	waywisa.
they	melon	eating-while	walking

'They are eating melon while walking.'

The other modes used the same ending with singular or plural verbs.

All of the endings given above are used to link verbs that have the same subject. If two verbs have different subjects, they may be joined by -qw, the different subject marker.

Pam meloonit tuumyta-qw wayma.
'S/he is eating melon while (someone else) is walking.'
Pam tiimayi-qw nima.
'S/he watched the dance and (someone else) went home.'
Pam nima-qw mangu'i.
'S/he went home and/ because someone got tired.'
Nu' pangso pitu-qw nösni.
'If I go there, someone else will eat.'

Specific meanings (such as 'if', 'because', etc.) must be inferred from context when using the different subject marker.

The Hopi word for 'not' is *qa*. It may precede any part of a sentence (object or verb, but not subject). In English, 'not' may only be used with verbs.

Pam	sikwit	qa	tuumoyta.
S/he	meat	not	be eating.

'S/he is not eating (the) meat.'

Pam	qa	sikwit	tuumoyta.
S/he	not	meat	be eating.

'It is not meat that s/he is eating.'

Note how the second sentence has an equivalent in English, although the object is not negated directly as in the Hopi sentence.

In Hopi, questions are formed by putting the particle *ya* in front of a sentence.

Pam	meloonit	tuumoyta.
S/he	melon	eating.

'She is eating melon.'

Ya	pam	meloonit	tuumoyta?
Question	s/he	melon	eating.

'Is s/he eating melon?'

Notice that the SOV (subject-object-verb) order remains in both sentences. Compare the two English sentences below:

The boy likes watermelons.
The boys like watermelon.

In English the difference between a single item (**singular** number) and more than one of the same item (**plural** number) is shown by adding the ending -*s* to either a noun or verb.

In Hopi, there are singular nouns and verbs; there are also plurals (to be discussed below). There is also a **dual** number.

Tiyo	nuy	siivat	maqa.
Boy	me	money	gave.

'The boy gave me (the) money.'

Tiyot   nuy   siivat   maqa.
'The two boys gave me (the) money.'

Pam   nuy   siivat   maqa.
'S/he gave me the money.'

Puma   nuy   siivat   maqa.
'The two of them gave me (the) money.'

In the second sentence, the subject has the ending -t; do not confuse this with the object marker -t or the mode -t ('then'). This is because the dual ending (for subjects) is -t. In the fourth example, the plural pronoun *puma* 'they' is used with a singular verb (the plural of *maqa* is *maqaya*).

To make a dual sentence, then, one does one of two things: (a) put the ending -t on the subject (if the subject is a noun), or else (b) use a plural pronoun as the subject.

The possibility exists, of course, of using a dual noun or pronoun as an object.

Tiyo   sinot   tuwa.
Boy   person   saw/found.
'The boy found/saw (a/the) person.'

Tiyot   sinot   tuwa.
'The two boys saw the person.'

Tiyo   sinotuy   tuwa.
'The boy saw the two people.'

Tiyot   sinotuy   tuwa.
'The two boys saw the two persons.'

Notice that the objective form of the dual ending is -tuy.

In Hopi there are three **tenses** (relative time an action takes place).

Pam   tiyo   nima.
That   boy   go home.
'That boy goes home' OR 'That boy went home.'

Pam	tiyo	qaavo	nima-ni.
That	boy	tomorrow	go-home-will.

'That boy will go home tomorrow.'

Pam	tiyo	talavay	nima-ngwu.
That	boy	mornings	go-home-usually.

'That boy usually/habitually goes home of a morning.'

To indicate the **future tense**, all you have to do is add -*ni* to the verb of a sentence. To indicate habitual or perpetual actions or states, one adds the ending -*ngwu* (the **habitual tense** marker) to the verb. There are no exceptions to the formation of tenses in Hopi, as there are in English and other European languages.

The simple form of the verb (for example: *maqa*, 'give/gave,' *tuwa*, 'see/saw,' *yori*, 'look/looked') can mean either past or present time. The exact meaning must be supplied from context by common sense.

In Hopi, nouns may have singular, dual and plural forms. Hopi nouns form plurals in one of five ways.

add -m
add -t, lengthen the preceding vowel, add falling tone
double the first syllable reduplication
double and add -m
double and add -t

Here are examples of how this works.

	Singular	Plural
person	sino	sinom
Hopi	Hopi	Hopìit
house	kiihu	kiikihu
child	tsay	tsaatsayom
girl	maana	mamant

Despite differences in the length of the first vowel, the plural forms are predictable. In fact, there are only two irregular plurals in the entire language (*tiyo*, 'boy,' *tootim*, 'boys,' *wùuti*, 'woman,' *momo'yam*, 'women').

If a plural noun is used as an object, if it ends in -t or -m, -uy is added to the ending (producing -tuy and -muy, respectively). In the case of nouns that double their first syllable for plural (all of which refer to inanimate things), the object marker -t is added.

In Hopi, if the subject is plural (three or more in number), the verb must be marked to show that the subject is plural. There are several ways in which this can be done. One is to double the first consonant of the verb.

| nima | go home | becomes | ninma (pl.) |
| tuwa | find | | tutwa (pl.) |

Some verbs change their form entirely to form a plural, such as the following pairs:

| yama | exit | becomes | nönga (pl.) |
| qatu | sit, stay | | yeese (pl.) |

Most Hopi verbs, however, have predictable or recognizable plural forms. Most verbs have distinctive endings that have singular and plural forms.

	Singular	Plural
become	-ti	-toti
go along doing	-ma	-wis(a)
go to do	-to	-wis(a)
be doing	-law(u)	-lalwa
did	-ta	-tota
have	-'yta	-'gyungwa
be in state of	-iwta	-iwyungwa

If a verb doesn't use any of these means of forming its plural, then it adds the ending -ya. Thus, if you are reading a text, in most instances you will be able to recognize a plural verb and then look it up, just as you are able to figure out the singular forms of Hopi nouns. (The vowels in parentheses are dropped if another ending is added.)

In Hopi the pronouns (words that stand in place of nouns such as 'I' and 'she') are similar to their English counterparts.

English	Hopi
I	nu'
me	nuy
thou	um
thee	ung
we	itam
us	itamuy
you	uma
ye	umuy

When marking ownership, Hopi is different from English.

English	Hopi
my	i-
thy	ùu-
our	ita(à)-
your	umu(ù)

In Hopi, the possessor markers are added to the noun they go with; the equivalents of 'our' and 'your (pl.)' may or may not have a long vowel with falling tone.

Hopi doesn't have any exact equivalents for *he, she, it,* and *they.* Instead, **demonstratives** (words like *this* and *that*) are used in their place.

English	Hopi
this	i'
that	pam
these	ima
those	puma

The words *pam* and *puma* are the most often used for the English words *he, she, it,* and *they.*

Hopi demonstratives have objective forms, which their English equivalents lack.

subjective	objective
i'	it
ima	imuy

pam	put
puma	pumuy

Some of these forms have already been encountered; they are all very common. (The term **subjective** is used in language description to refer to the subject forms of nouns and pronouns.)

The Hopi equivalents of *her, his, its,* and *their* are endings that are attached to nouns.

her/his/its	-'at
their	-'am

Consider the following words:

paasa'at	her/his/its field
paasa'am	their field

When these are used as objects, the accusative forms used are: *-yat* and *-yamuy*.

TECHNICAL GLOSSARY

Augmentation
in music, slowing the speed by about half

Coda
1. formal ending (ex. *Amen* at the end of a prayer in English) 2. in music, and rarely in Hopi stories, a closing section

Contrastive mechanism
a narrative technique that highlights a line or word

Deictic
a word that points out another word or expression (ex. *this, that, the*)

Deictic sectioning
in Hopi traditional narratives and orations, the use of **proximal** or **distal** reference to group the lines of a story into sections

Desire function
see **narrative schema**

Diminution
speeding up the **tempo** of a piece of music to about twice the original speed

Discourse topic
the theme(s) that serve as the main idea(s) of a section or entire discourse; in Hopi discourse, these are marked by proximals on first mention in a section.

Distal
a pointing word (**deictic**) that refers to space away from the speaker and possibly addressee (ex. *that, there*)

Distal reference
use of a **distal** to mark the remention of a section or discourse topic (first mention in Hopi traditional narratives is with a **proximal** reference)

Domain
with respect to quotations, the length/amount of text to which a **quotative** particle applies

Evaluation section
a section of a text or performance that generates interest and shows that the performance or text is a valid example of its **genre** (ex. the lesson at the end of a fable)

Evaluative device
any **paralinguistic feature** that underscores the value of a performance or text (ex. drawing out the word *biggest* in: *that's the biggest* _____ *I ever saw!*)

Exclusive
with pronouns, the exclusion of the person spoken to (ex. *The two of us are getting married on Tuesday*, spoken to a third party); see **inclusive**

Flat text
a written text with no indication of intonation, pausing, or loudness

Formulaic expression
a phrase in a language that is fixed, and which is a vocabulary item just like a single word (ex. *tried and true, rain cats and dogs*)

Function
steps in the action of a story; see **narrative schema**

Gaze
in conversation, the gaze and maintaining eye contact

Genre
broadly, a kind of verbal art in a typical context; more strictly, a kind of discourse that is named and which has specified characteristics

Genre signature
a feature (phonological, grammatical, lexical) that is not only typical of a **genre**, but which must be present (ex. *amen* at the end of a prayer)

Hemiola
in music, the shift from a pulse of two (ONE-two) to a pulse of three (ONE-two-three); in Hopi music, the three beats of a hemiola receive about the same loudness; see **meter**

Inclusive
in pronouns, the inclusion of the person spoken to (ex. in the sentence *let's the two of us go grab a bit to eat*, the person addressed is included; see **exclusive**)

Indirection
use of words other than "you"

Interlude
in music or literature, a relatively short section that bridges two major sections

Intertextuality
the association of related texts in terms of content and/or form

Journey function
see **narrative schema**

Kinesic
refers to use of body movement and gesture for communicative purposes

Line
a unit of language, usually a simple sentence in length (subject plus verb or other predicate) which receives a typical intonation pattern, and which is separated from other lines by pausing (ex. commas are used to distinguish line in poetry in English: *roses are red, violets are blue*)

Local topic chain
a series of topics marked in the same way (in Hopi narratives, this is usually with the suffix *-wa*, which may connect items several lines apart), momentarily highlights a series of items or actions within a single section

Meter
in music and some poetry, the gathering of pulses into groups of the same pattern (ex. ONE-two-three in waltz time)

Narrative clause
in Hopi traditional narratives, a clause where a character is not talking; it does not contain a **quotative** particle

Narrative schema
the overall way a story is supposed to be told; in Hopi narratives, the story is always cast as a journey away from a home base; the parts of the story include: **setting, desire** (of the protagonist), her/his **plan** of action, a **journey**, and the **outcome**; these steps in the action are called **functions**

Overlap
where the syntactic and intonation lines of a discourse do not match (ex. in English conversation, a speaker may return to a topic after being disturbed or interrupted by using the word *so: so this guy was out walking his dog* returns to the topic of taking a dog for a walk)

Paralinguistic feature
a feature of speaking that is not purely language, which is used to communicate mood, urgency, etc. (ex. loudness, relative speed of talking, humming words to indicate discretion)

Pausal
in Hopi grammar, the copying of a vowel of a word (most Hopi words end in a vowel); with nouns and pronouns, this makes the noun or pronoun a predicate (ex. *nu'*, 'I,' becomes *nu'u*, 'it is me'); with verbs, it creates a command (ex. *nöösa*, 'ate it,' becomes *nöösa'a*); with words ending in a consonant, the pausal form is not predictable (ex. *lavaytatampit akw peena*, 'wrote it with a typewriter' becomes *lavaytatampit akw'a* as a response to a question)

Pausalization
the process or use of **pausals**

Plan function
see **narrative schema**

Proximal
a word that refers to relative nearness to the speaker (and possibly addressee; ex. *this, here*)

Proximal reference
use of a **proximal** in a narrative or oration to mark the first mention in a text of a discourse **topic**; see **deictic, distal**

Quatrain
a grouping of lines into four sequential lines for rhetorical effect

Quotation
distinct from a **quotative clause** (which has a **quotative particle**), a quotation in a Hopi traditional narrative does not have a quotative particle in it; rather, it is framed by a verb of speaking ('say,' 'tell,' 'ask,' etc.) and by the verb *kita*, 'state' at the end

Quotative clause
in Hopi traditional narratives, a clause which contains the particle *yaw*, 'it is said/they say'; technically, a quotative should appear in all clauses except those where characters speak (**narrative clauses**)

Quotative particle
the Hopi word *yaw* which indicates that the speaker (storyteller) did not experience directly what s/he is talking about; in stories, this particle is used throughout to indicate that the story is hearsay; see **quotative clause**

Realization function
see **narrative schema**

Regulatory mechanisms
intonations and pausing used to shape the flow and pace of a verbal discourse.

Remention
mention of a character, prop, or place again in the same section of a story or oration (ex. in English, *she* or *he* is often used to mark rementions, but in Hopi the distal *pam*, 'that one,' is used)

RHF intonation sequence
an intonation contour with a rise-hold-falling pattern, typical of Hopi announcements and oration

Scansion
criteria for grouping lines into a pattern

Setting
see **narrative schema**

songpoem
a kind of Hopi song that is AABBA in form, and which is composed for public events; this is the form that poetry takes in Hopi culture (a poem must be enveloped in music)

Spatial deixis
word or expression that indicates space or location (ex. *here, there*)

Style
the distinctive manner of composing and structuring a piece of discourse (ex. compare the wording of telegrams and the wording of the article that follows)

Tempo
the relative speed of a piece of music

Temporal deixis
a word or expression that indicates a particular time (ex. *now, then, yesterday*)

Theme
narrowly, an idea which serves as one of the relatively few topics in a Hopi traditional announcement or prayer

Tone cluster
the use of a group of tones to punctuate or accompany a piece of music (ex. chords in western music)

Tonic
the primary reference pitch in a piece of music

Topic
what a piece of literature is about; there may be sectional topics as opposed to discourse topics; see **local topic chain**

Validation
a section or device that insures the fitness of a text or performance as an example of its genre (ex. the abbreviated list of ingredients at the beginning of a recipe)

Versification
hierarchical organization of the lines of a text into groupings according to a **scansion** convention

Vocable
a syllable or word which has an emotional impact as its primary meaning rather than a literal meaning (ex. *tralala* has no exact meaning, but connotes lightness, even frivolity)

Volume topic
a topic defined by an increase of loudness

BIBLIOGRAPHY

Bahr, Donald M. 1975. *Pima and Papago ritual oratory: a study of three texts.* San Francisco: Indian Historian Press.

Baker, Theodore. 1978 [1882]. *On the music of the North American Indians.* Trans. by Ann Buckley. New York: DaCapo. [originally published in German]

Bauman, Richard. 1986. *Story, performance, event.* Cambridge: Cambridge University Press.

Black, Mary E. 1984. Maidens and mothers: an analysis of Hopi corn metaphors. *Ethnology* 23:279–88.

Black, Robert A. 1964. A content analysis of 81 Hopi Indian chants. Ph.D. diss., Indiana University.

———. 1967a. Hopi grievance chants: a mechanism of social control. In *Studies in Southwestern Ethnolinguistics,* ed. by D. H. Hymes and W. E. Bittle, 54–67. The Hague: Mouton.

———. 1967b. Hopi rabbit-hunt chants: A ritualized language. In *Essays on the verbal and visual arts,* ed. by J. H. McNeish, 7–11. Seattle: American Ethnological Society and University of Washington Press.

Brenneis, Donald. 1986. Shared territory: Audience, indirection, and meaning. *Text* 6:339–47.

Bright, William R. 1979. A Karok myth in "measured verse": The translation of a performance. *Journal of California and Great Basin Research* 1:117–1123.

Bunzel, Ruth. 1932. Singing and dancing. In *Introduction to Zuni ceremonialism.* Bureau of American Ethnology, Annual Report 47: 474–544.

Burlin, Natalie. See "Curtis, Natalie."

Chesky, Jane. 1941. Indian music of the Southwest. *The Kiva* 7:9–12.

Courlander, Harold. 1971. *The fourth world of the Hopis.* New York: Crown Publishers.

Curtis, Natalie. 1903. An American Indian composer. *Harper's* [Monthly] 107(1140):626–31.

————. 1906. Isleta hunting song. *Southern Workman* 35:144.

————. 1907. *The Indians' Book.* New York: Harper and Brothers.

————. 1921. American Indian cradle songs. *Musical Quarterly* 7:549–58.

Densmore, Frances. 1938. Music of Santo Domingo Pueblo. *Southwest Museum Papers* 12.

————. 1950. The words of Indian songs as unwritten literature. *Journal of American Folklore* 63:450–58.

————. 1957. Music of Acoma, Isleta, Cochiti and Zuni Pueblos. Bureau of American Ethnology, *Bulletin* 165.

Dozier, Edward P. 1970. *The Pueblo Indians of North America.* New York: Holt, Rinehart and Winston.

Dubois, John. 1987. The discourse basis of ergativity. *Language* 63:805–55.

Eco, Umberto. 1979. *The Role of the reader.* Bloomington: Indiana University Press.

Evans, Bessie, and May G. Evans. 1931. *American Indian dance steps.* New York: A. S. Barnes.

Fewkes, Jesse Walter. 1902. Minor Hopi festivals. *American Anthropologist* 4:482–511.

Fillmore, John C. 1894. A study of Indian music. *The Century Magazine* 47:616–23.

————. 1896. Two Tigua folk-songs. *Land of Sunshine* [Los Angeles] 4:273–80.

————. 1897. The forms spontaneously assumed by folk-songs. *Music* 12:289–94.

Frisbie, Charlotte J. 1977. *Music and dance research of the Southwestern United States.* Detroit: Information Coordinators.

Garcia, Antonio, and Carlos Garcia. 1968. Ritual preludes to Tewa dances. *Ethnomusicology* 1:239–44.

Geertz, Armin, and Michael Lomatuwa'yma. 1987. *Children of cottonwood: Piety and ceremonialism in Hopi Indian puppetry.* Lincoln: University of Nebraska Press.

Gilman, Benjamin Ives. 1891. Zuni melodies. *Journal of American Ethnology and Archaeology* 1:65–91.

————. 1908. Hopi songs. *Journal of American Ethnology and Archaeology* 5:1–226.

————. 1909. The science of exotic music. *Science* 30:532–35.

Goldfrank, Esther S. 1923. Notes on two Pueblo feasts. *American Anthropologist* 25:188–96.

Hanks, William F. 1987. Discourse genres in a theory of practice. *American Ethnologist* 14:668–92.

Herzog, George. 1935. Special song types in North American Indian music. *Zeitschrift für Vergleichenden Musikwissenschaft* 3:23–33.

————. 1936. A comparison of Pueblo and Pima musical styles. *Journal of American Folklore* 49:283–417.

Hopi Gospel songs for church and street services. 1921. (n.p.): Mennonite and Baptist Mission Boards.

Hough, Walter. 1897. Music of the Hopi Flute Ceremony. *American Anthropologist* 10:162–63.

Hymes, Dell. 1981. *"In vain I tried to tell you": Essays in Native American ethnopoetics.* Philadelphia: University of Pennsylvania Press.

———. 1987. Tonkawa poetics: John Rush Buffalo's "Coyote and Eagle's daughters." In *Native American discourse*, ed. by J. Sherzer and T Woodbury, 17–61. London: Cambridge University Press.

———. 1992. Helen Sekaquaptewa's "Coyote and the birds": Rhetorical analysis of a Hopi Coyote story. *Anthropological Linguistics* 34:45–72.

———. 1994. Ethnopoetics, oral formulaic theory, and editing texts. *Oral Tradition* 9(2): 330–60.

———. 1995. Reading Takelma texts: Francis Johnson's "Coyote and the Frog." In R. D. Abrahams, ed., *Fields of folklore: Essays in honor of Kenneth S. Goldstein*. Bloomington, Ind.: Trickster Press.

Hymes, Virginia. 1987. Warm Springs Sahaptin narrative analysis. In *Native American discourse: Poetics and rhetoric*, ed. by J. Sherzer and A. C. Woodbury, 62–102. London: Cambridge University Press.

James, Harry C. 1974. *Pages from Hopi history*. Tucson: University of Arizona Press.

Jeancon, Jean A. 1924. *Indian song book*. Denver: Denver Art Museum.

Kabotie, Mike, ed. 1978. *Two Hopi song poets of Shongopavi*. n.p.: n.p.

Kennard, Edward. 1989. Honanyestiwa and Honanyesnöma: A visit to the underworld. *Tlalocan* 11:149–72.

Kintsh, W., and E. Greene. 1978. The role of culture-specific schemata in comprehension and recall of stories. *Discourse Processes* 1:1–13.

Koike, Dale A. 1989. Requests and the role of deixis in politeness. *Journal of Pragmatics* 13:187–202.

Kroskrity, Paul V. 1985. Growing on stories: Lines, verse and genre in an Arizona Tewa text. *Journal of Anthropological Research* 41:183–99.

———. 1992. Arizona Tewa announcements: Form, function and linguistic ideology. *Anthropological Linguistics* 34:104–16.

———. 1993. *Language, history and identity: Ethnolinguistic studies of the Arizona Tewa*. Tucson: University of Arizona Press.

Kurath, Gertrude Prokosch. 1957. Dance styles of the Rio Grande Pueblo Indians. *The Folklorist* 4:89.

———. 1958. Buffalo dances at Cochiti Pueblo. *The Folklorist* 4:149–50.

———. 1959. Cochiti choreographies and songs. In *Cochiti: A New Mexican Pueblo, past and present*, by C. H. Lange, 539–56. Carbondale: Southern Illinois University Press.

———. 1960. Calling the rain gods. *Journal of American Folklore* 73:312–16.

———. 1962. American Indian dances: Rituals for sustenance. *The Folklorist* 7:8–11.

———. 1965. Tewa choreographic music. In *Studies in ethnomusicology*, ed. by M. Kolinski, 2:4–19.

———. 1969. A comparison of Plains and Pueblo style. *Ethnomusicology* 13:512–17.

Kurath, Gertrude Prokosch, and Antonio Garcia. 1969. *Music and dance of the Tewa pueblos*. Santa Fe: Museum of New Mexico Press.

Kurzon, Dennis. 1985. Signposts for the reader: A corpus-based study of text deixis. *Text* 5:187–200.

Labov, William, and Joshua Waletsky. 1967. Narrative analysis: Oral versions of personal experience. In *Essays on the verbal and visual arts*, ed. by June Helm, 12–24. Seattle: American Ethnological Society and University of Washington Press.

Laird, W. David. 1977. *Hopi Bibliography.* Tucson: University of Arizona Press.

Lange, Charles H. 1959. *Cochiti: A New Mexican Pueblo past and present.* Carbondale: Southern Illinois University Press.

Lauerbach, Gerda. 1989. "We don't want war, but . . .": Speech act schemata and inter-schema inference transfer. *Journal of Pragmatics* 13:25–51.

Leslie, Ebin. 1984. Keynote address. In *Report of the Third Hopi Mental Health Conference: Prophecy in motion*, ed. by Hopi Health Department, 36–40. Kykotsmovi, Ariz.: Hopi Health Department, The Hopi Tribe.

Lewis, Herman. 1984. Keynote address. In *Report of the Third Hopi Mental Health Conference: Prophecy in motion*, 24–29. Kykotsmovi, Ariz.: Hopi Health Department, The Hopi Tribe.

List, George. 1962. Songs in Hopi culture, past and present. International Folk Music Conference, *Journal* 14:30–35.

———. 1964. The Hopi and the White Man's music. *Sing Out* 14(2):47–49.

———. 1967. The Hopi as composer and poet. Centennial Workshop on Ethnomusicology, *Proceedings*, 43–53. Vancouver: University of British Columbia.

———. 1985. Hopi melodic concepts. *Journal of the American Musicological Society* 38(1):143–52.

———. 1987. Stability and variation in a Hopi lullaby. *Ethnomusicology* 31:18–34.

———. 1993. *Stability and Variation in Hopi Song.* Philadelphia: American Philosophical Society.

Lomaquahu, Percy. 1985. [Keynote address]. In *Report of the Fourth Hopi Mental Health Conference: Happiness, health and peace*, 40–45, Kykotsmovi, Ariz.: Hopi Health Department, The Hopi Tribe.

Lomatuwa'yma, Michael, Lorena Lomatuwa'yma, and Sidney Namingha. 1994. *Hopi ruin legends: Kiqötutuwutsi.* Ed. by E. Malotki. Lincoln: University of Nebraska Press.

Lomatuwa'yma, Michael, Lorena Lomatuwa'yma, Sidney Namingha, Leslie Koyawena, and Herschel Talashoma. 1995. *The Bedbugs' night dance and other Hopi sexual tales: Mumuspi'yyungqa tuutuwutsi.* Ed. by E. Malotki. Lincoln: University of Nebraska Press.

Lomayaktewa, Starlie. 1985. [Opening remarks]. In *Report of the Fourth Hopi Mental Health Conference: Happiness, health and peace*, 15–18, Kykotsmovi, Ariz.: Hopi Health Department, The Hopi Tribe.

MacLeish, Kenneth. 1941. A few Hopi songs from Moenkopi. *Masterkey* 15:178–84.

Malotki, Ekkehart, ed. 1978. *Hopitutuwutsi: Hopi tales.* Flagstaff, Ariz.: Museum of Northern Arizona Press.

Malotki, Ekkehart, and Michael Lomatuwa'yma, eds. 1984. *Hopi Coyote stories.* Lincoln: University of Nebraska Press.

——. 1985. *Gullible Coyote: Una'ihu*. Tucson: University of Arizona Press.

——. 1987a. *Stories of Maasaw, a Hopi god*. Lincoln: University of Nebraska Press.

——. 1987b. *Maasaw: Profile of a Hopi God*. Lincoln: University of Nebraska Press.

——. 1987c. *Earth fire: A legend of the Sunset Crater eruption*. Flagstaff, Ariz.: Northland Press.

Marshall, Alfred, ed. and trans. 1975. *Interlinear Greek-English New Testament: The new international version*. Grand Rapids, Mich.: Zondervan Publishing House.

McAllester, David P. 1961. *Indian music of the Southwest*. Colorado Springs: Taylor Museum.

McLeod, Norma. 1974. Ethnomusicology. *Annual Review of Anthropology* 2:99–115.

McNutt, James C. 1984. John Comfort Fillmore: A student of Indian music reconsidered. *American Music* 2:61–70.

Nettl, Bruno. 1954. North American Indian musical styles. *Memoirs of the American Folklore Society* 45.

New Testament [Hopi]. 1983. *God lavayiyat ang puhuvasiwni*. New York: American Bible Society.

Ochs, Elinor. 1979. Planned and unplanned discourse. In *Discourse and syntax*, ed. by Talmy Givón, 51–80. (Syntax and Semantics 12). New York: Academic Press.

Ortiz, Alfonso. 1969. A uniquely American legacy. *Princeton University Library Journal* 30(3):147–57.

Ortiz, Alfonso, ed. 1979. *Southwest handbook of North American Indians* 9. Washington, D.C.: Smithsonian Institution Press.

Ortiz, Simon. 1977. *Song, poetry and language: Expression and perception*. [Tsaile, Ariz.]: Navajo Community College Press.

Parsons, Elsie Clewes. 1925. *A Pueblo Indian journal, 1920–1921. Memoirs of the American Anthropological Society* 32.

——. 1939. *Pueblo Indian religion*. Chicago: University of Chicago Press. 2 volumes.

Postal, Susan K. 1965. Body-image and identity: A comparison of Kwakiutl and Hopi. *American Anthropologist* 67:455–62.

Pratt, Mary L. 1977. *Towards a speech act theory of literary discourse*. Bloomington: Indiana University Press.

Rhodes, Robert W. 1972. Selected Hopi secular music: Transcription and analysis. Ph.D. diss., Arizona State University.

——. 1977. *Hopi music and dance*. Tsaile, Ariz.: Navajo Community College Press.

Rice, E. G. 1980. On cultural schemata. *American Ethnologist* 7:152–72.

Roberts, Don L. 1972. The ethnomusicology of the Eastern Pueblos. In *New Perspectives on the Pueblos*, ed. by A. Ortiz, 243–56. Albuquerque: University of New Mexico Press.

Roberts, Helen H. 1927. Indian music from the Southwest. *Natural History* 27(3):257–65.

——. 1928. Analysis of Picuris song. In *Picuris children's songs with texts and stories*, 399–47. *Annual Reports of the Bureau of American Ethnology* 43:289–447.

——. 1936a. *Musical areas in aboriginal North America*. Yale University Publications in Anthropology 12.

――. 1936b. Chakwena songs of Zuni and Laguna. *Journal of American Folklore* 36:177–84.

Rosenberg, Bruce A. 1970. *The art of the American folk preacher.* New York: Oxford University Press.

Sands, Kathleen, and Emory Sekaquaptewa. 1978. Four Hopi lullabies: A study in method and meaning. *American Indian Quarterly* 4(3):195–210.

Sekaquaptewa, Emory. 1985 Keynote address. In *Report of the Fourth Hopi Mental Health Conference: Happiness, health and peace,* 19–27, Kykotsmovi, Ariz.: Hopi Health Department, The Hopi Tribe.

Sekaquaptewa, Helen. 1978. Iisaw: Hopi Coyote stories. In *Words and Place* 4, prod. by Larry Evers. New York: Clearwater Publications.

Seumptewa, E., C. F. Voegelin, and F. M. Voegelin. 1980. Wren and Coyote. In *Coyote stories* 2, ed. by Martha B. Kendall, 104–10. *International Journal of American Linguistics, Native American Text Series* 6. Chicago: University of Chicago Press.

Shaul, David L. Commentary. In Voth n.d.

――. 1987a. Pragmatic constraints on Hopi narrative discourse. Berkeley Linguistic Society, *Proceedings* 13:263–69.

――. 1987b. Cohesion in Hopi narratives. Proceedings of the First International Pragmatics Conference, ed. by J. Verschueren, 579–84. Amsterdam: John Benjamins.

――. 1988. A Hopi radio commercial. *International Journal of American Linguistics* 54:96–105.

――. 1992. A Hopi songpoem in "context." In *On the translation of Native American literature.* Washington, D.C.: Smithsonian Institution Press.

――. 1994. Two Hopi songpoems. In B. Swann, ed., *Coming to light: Contemporary translations of Native literatures of North America,* 679–89. New York: Random House.

Shaul, David L., R. Albert, C. Golstan, and R. Satory. 1987. The Hopi Coyote story as narrative: The problem of evaluation. *Journal of Pragmatics* 11:17–39.

Sidney, Ivan. 1985. [Opening remarks]. In *Report of the Fourth Hopi Mental Health Conference: Happiness, health and peace,* 12–14, Kykotsmovi, Ariz.: Hopi Health Department, The Hopi Tribe.

Spinden, Herbert J. 1917. Indian dances of the Southwest. *Scientific American,* Supplement 2140:8–9.

――. 1931. *Songs of the Tewa.* New York: Exposition of Indian Tribal Arts.

Stephen, Alexander M. 1936. *Hopi journal.* Ed. by E. C. Parsons. Columbia University Contributions to Anthropology 23. 2 vols.

Sweet, Jill Drayson. 1983. Ritual and theatre in Tewa ceremonial performances. *Ethnomusicology* 9:253–69.

Tedlock, Barbara. 1980. Song of the Zuni Kachina Society: Composition, rehearsal, and performance. In *Southwestern Indian ritual drama,* ed. by C. J. Frisbie, 1–35. Albuquerque: University of New Mexico Press.

Tedlock, Dennis. 1983. *The spoken word and the work of interpretation.* Philadelphia: University of Pennsylvania Press.

Thompson, Laura, and Alice Joseph. 1944. *The Hopi way.* Chicago: University of Chicago Press.

Titiev, Mischa. 1944. *Old Oraibi: A study of the Hopi Indians of Third Mesa.* Cambridge, Mass.: Peabody Museum, Harvard University.

Urban, G. 1986. Ceremonial dialogues in South America. *American Anthropologist* 88:371–386.

Ushie, Yukio. 1986. Corepresentation: A textual function of indefinite expressions. *Text* 6:427–46.

Van Stone, Mary R. 1941. Song of the Indians. *El Palacio* 48:149–54.

Voegelin, Carl F., and Robert C. Euler. 1957. Introduction to Hopi chants. *Journal of American Folklore* 70:115–36.

Voth Henry R. n.d. [The Hopi Prose Texts of H. R. Voth.] Ms., Mennonite Library and Archives. North Newton, Kans.: Bethel College.

Whiteley, Peter. 1988. *Bacavi: Journey to Reed Springs.* Flagstaff, Ariz.: Northland Press.

Wiget, Andrew. 1987. Telling the tale: A performance analysis of a Hopi Coyote story. In *Recovering the word: Essays on Native American literature,* ed. by B. Swann and A. Krupat, 297–336. Berkeley: University of California Press.

Williams, James R. 1948. Tribal education of the Hopi Indian. Master's thesis, Arizona State College (Flagstaff).

Woodbury, Anthony C. 1987. Rhetorical structure in a Central Alaskan Yupik Eskimo traditional narrative. In *Native American discourse: Poetics and rhetoric,* ed. by Joel Sherzer and Anthony C. Woodbury, 176–239. London: Cambridge University Press.

INDEX

Numbers in italics refer to tables.

admonitions and proverbs, 6, 14, 118,
139–40, 151, 152–53; expressed in
negative form, 154; statement of
prohibition and statement of
consequences, 153
adverbial proforms, 156
Anasazi, 12–13
announcements, 6, 9, 10, 14, 117, 119;
for ceramic art exhibit, 136; for
communal hunt, 132–35; cues
and, 125; and sectioning, 122;
structuring of, 16; thematic
foci of, 121; use of chains of
subordinate clauses in, 135; use
of third party, 122
Arizona State Museum, 136
Arizona Tewa language, 12, 17, 121
asides, 91, 92, 97; audience response
to, 93
audiences: cues for response from,
95–97, 160; interaction with
performer, 7–8, 10, 15, 23, 87, 159;
response and proximal markings,
96; response to asides, 93; response
to word order deviation, 96
augmentation, 176; defined, 216

ba (quotative particle), 17
Baker, Theodore, 173
Basket Dances, 185
Biblical narratives: adaptation of, 51–55
binary marking, 97
Bunzel, Ruth, 191
Burlin, Natalie Curtis, 173
Butterfly Dance, 203

caretaker speech, 144
ceramic art exhibit announcement, 136
chants, 14, 119; repetition in, 121; and
sermons, 125
Chinookan rhetorical pattern, 57
circumlocution, 138
codas (in literature), 90, 95, 130, 201;
defined, 216
codas (in music), 177, 178–80, 182, 196,
206; defined, 216; and social
dance songs, 180
communal hunt announcement, 132–35;
use of journey metaphor, 135
conflict: dealing with, 147
conjunctive verb endings, 201
contrastive mechanisms, 93; defined, 216
conversation, 119; and eye contact, 144;
as genre, 144, 160; idealized,
144–46, 160; lexical and

229

quatrains, 8, 9, 22, 56, 152, 157–59;
defined, 219; defined by
subordination, 91, 94, 96; and
extemporaneous performance,
84; interruption of, 92; issues
involving, 84–85; and "Lolenso,"
79–80; in New Testament translation, 81–82; verbal response to, 96
quotation: defined, 219
quotation clauses, 17
quotative clauses: defined, 219
quotative expressions: shared by two
lines, 92; used as genre signatures,
16; use in narrative clauses, 17
quotative particles, 8, 17; defined, 219
-qw (pausalization), 52–53, 157

rabbit hunt announcement. *See*
communal hunt announcement
radio commercial: text of, 125–29;
themes in, 129–30
Realization function, 78, 90
Realization sections, 94
regulatory mechanisms, 93; defined, 219
rementions, 134, 135, 151, 152, 155;
defined, 219
repetitions, 125; parallel, 124
rhetorical patterning, 58
Rhodes, Robert W., 178
rhythm, 176, 180, 188; duple, 196, 200,
201, 204; in social dances, 178; two
levels of, 177
riddles, 147
Rio Grande Tewa language, 12
Rise-Hold-Fall (RHF) intonation
contour, 9, 117, 122, 123–24, 125,
130, 137; defined, 220; as genre
signature of *tsa'alawu*, 136
rituals, 7; and song cycles, 186
ritual songs, 9; listed, 186
Roberts, Helen, 175, 176, 181

Santo Domingo Pueblo, 175

sayings, 14, 117, 148, 154
scales, musical, 173–75; lacking in Hopi
music, 180; pentatonic, 174;
question of innate or learned, 173
scansion, 22; and couplets, 64; defined,
220
scansion convention, 58–59
Science magazine, 174
"The Science of Exotic Music"
(Gilman), 174
Second Mesa texts, 48–51
sectioning, 16–23, 51, 155; deictically
defined, 159; and deictic marking,
51, 159; and journey metaphor, 21;
and narrative functions, 78–79;
and public announcements, 122;
two systems of, 56
Sekaquaptewa, Emory, 124, 136, 148, 189;
oration by, 161–71
Sekaquaptewa, Helen, 58, 86, 92
Setima, Ann Mae, 49
Setting, Desire, Plan, Journey,
Realization, 8, 18, 21, 89–90
Setting function, 89
Simpson, Louis, 57
singular number, 210
Smith, Hiram, 57
social dances, 14, 120, 178, 182; songs
used in, 180, 185
Social Darwinism, 173–75
songpoems, 9, 10, 14; analysis of, 201–6;
anatomy of, 178; composition of,
191; and corn metaphor, 189–90;
defined, 220; difference with
songs, 118, 172; as genre in Hopi
music, 187; kinds of, listed,
184; Korosta Kachina, 201; as
literature, 190; need to create new,
189, 191; parts of, 179; performance
of, 185–86; and social dance, 185;
subgenres of, 177–78; of Tewa
Indians, 182; themes in, 190; traits
of, 196